Haunted
Missouri

M000188994

0 11557 01014 5

Haunted
Missouri

**Ghosts and Strange Phenomena
of the Show Me State**

Troy Taylor
Illustrations by Marc Radle

STACKPOLE
BOOKS

Copyright ©2012 by Stackpole Books

Published by
STACKPOLE BOOKS
5067 Ritter Road
Mechanicsburg, PA 17055
www.stackpolebooks.com

All rights reserved, including the right to reproduce this book or portions thereof in any form or by any means, electronic or mechanical, including photocopying, recording, or by any information storage and retrieval system, without permission in writing from the publisher. All inquiries should be addressed to Stackpole Books.

Printed in the United States of America

10 9 8 7 6 5 4 3 2 1

FIRST EDITION
Cover design by Tessa J. Sweigert

Library of Congress Cataloging-in-Publication Data

Taylor, Troy.
  Haunted Missouri : ghosts & strange phenomena of the Show Me State / Troy Taylor. — 1st ed.
      p. cm.
  Includes bibliographical references (p.   ).
  ISBN 978-0-8117-1014-5 (pbk.)
  1. Ghosts—Missouri. 2. Haunted places—Missouri. I. Title.
  BF1472.U6T3965 2012
  133.109778—dc23

                                    2011038253

Contents

Introduction

AFTER VISITING MISSOURI, YOU CAN ALMOST UNDERSTAND WHY THE dead are so reluctant to leave.

It is a place of great diversity and amazing beauty, stretching from the Mississippi River to the forests and rolling hills of the Ozarks, with caves, rivers, and rugged woodland in between. The state is home to scores of ghostly tales, from documented hauntings to folk tales that have been passed along from one generation to the next. Missouri is also home to one of America's most haunted houses at one end of the state and one of the country's greatest unsolved mysteries at the other. Thanks to sites like those, along with countless stories that include wandering spirits, women in black, ghostly graveyards, haunted caves, lingering criminals, and much more, Missouri has always held great appeal for those with an interest in the macabre.

It is also a place where history has left its mark. There is a marked contrast between the cities of Missouri and the rural lands of the state, dating all the way back to the Civil War era when residents of St. Louis chose to remain loyal to the Union and the rest of the state sided with the Confederacy. As most readers know, a good ghost story cannot exist without great history behind it. The events of yesterday, it seems clear, are what create the hauntings of today.

But few volumes of history seem to capture the darker side of Missouri's past. Such tales, unknown to many readers, bring to life a side of the state that not everyone is familiar with. In the pages ahead, our trip into Missouri's past will also include the ghosts, haunted houses, strange events, bizarre legends, and bloody accounts that are often too unusual to be the stuff of your average history book.

Are such stories true? No one can say, but each of them was related to me, or documented, as being the truth. They were all real stories, told by real people, who believed in the truth behind what they experienced. The truth of each story is up to the reader to decide.

Just remember, to paraphrase the famous line, there are stranger things on earth than are dreamt of in our philosophies. Some of these strange things are lurking—perhaps just around the next corner—in the haunted state of Missouri.

Spirits of St. Louis

The Lemp Mansion

In 1929, Gerald Holland wrote in *American Mercury* magazine that "whatever odium may be attached to beer in other parts of the Republic, its status in St. Louis is as firmly grounded as James Eads' span across the Mississippi . . . beer made St. Louis."

And he was right. Beer was the lifeblood of St. Louis for decades, especially after the arrival of thousands of German settlers in the 1830s. They wanted beer and were determined to have it, creating brewing empires whose memories still linger today.

The Lemp family came to prominence in the middle 1800s as one of the premier brewing families of St. Louis. For years, they were the fiercest rival of Anheuser-Busch and the first makers of lager beer in middle America, but today they are largely forgotten and remembered more for the house they built than for the beer they once brewed. That house stands now as a fitting memorial to their decadence, wealth, and tragedy. Perhaps because of this tragedy, there is a sadness that hangs over the place and an eerie feeling that has remained from its days of disrepair and abandonment. It has since been restored into a restaurant and inn, but the sorrow seems to remain. By day, the mansion is a bustling restaurant, filled with people and activity, but at night, after everyone is gone and the doors have been locked tight, something still walks the halls of the Lemp Mansion.

The story of the Lemp brewing empire began in 1836 when Johann Adam Lemp came to America from Germany. He lived for a time in Cincinnati and then moved west to St. Louis. In 1838, he opened a small mercantile store at what is now Delmar and Sixth Streets, where, in addition to common household items, he sold vinegar and beer that he made himself. Both items were soon in great demand and he opened a small plant and offered beer from a pub that was attached to the factory. During this time, Adam introduced to St. Louis one of the first lager beers in America. This new beer was a great change from the English-style ales that had previously been popular, and the lighter beer soon became a regional favorite. Business prospered and by 1845 the popularity of the beer was enough to allow Adam to discontinue vinegar production and concentrate solely on beer.

The company expanded rapidly, thanks to demand for the beer. Needing a larger operation, plus a cool location to lager (store for a time) the beer, Adam purchased land above a limestone cave south of the city. The cave, which was located at the present-day corner of Cherokee and De Menil Place, could be kept cool by chopping ice from the nearby Mississippi River and depositing it inside. Adam excavated and expanded the cave to make room for the wooden beer casks and soon the new company was in operation. The Lemp Western Brewing Company grew throughout the 1840s and within a few years became one of the largest breweries in the city.

Adam Lemp went from a poor immigrant to one of the most respected men in St. Louis. He died in August 1862 and left his thriving business in the hands of his son, William. Under William's leadership, the brewery began to grow in ways that Adam could never have conceived of.

William Lemp had been born in Germany in 1836, just before his parents came to America. He spent his childhood in Germany and was brought to St. Louis by his father at age twelve. After graduating from St. Louis University, he joined his father at Western Brewery. At the outbreak of the Civil War, he joined the military and served with the St. Louis Home Guard, which was pro-Union. He was mustered out after taking part in the defense of the St. Louis Arsenal. Soon after, he married Julia Feickert; the couple would have nine children together.

After his father's death, William began to expand the brewery. He purchased a five-block area around the storage house on Cherokee, which was located above the lagering caves, and began the construction of a new brewery complex. By the 1870s, the Lemp factory was believed to be the largest in the entire city. A bottling plant was added in 1877 and artificial refrigeration was installed one year later. Lemp had a fascination with progress and new inventions and constantly updated the operation.

By the middle 1890s, the Lemp brewery was becoming known all over America. Its most popular line, Falstaff, became a favorite across the country, something that had never been accomplished by a regional brewery before. Lemp was the first brewery to establish coast-to-coast distribution of its beer, shipping it out in refrigerated railroad cars. After expanding across America, Lemp also spread to overseas markets and by the late 1890s, the beer could be found in Canada, Mexico, Britain, Germany, Central and South America, the West Indies, the Hawaiian Islands, Australia, Japan, and beyond. The brewery, ranked as the eighth largest in the country, had grown to the point that it employed more than seven hundred men; as many as one hundred horses were needed to pull the delivery wagons in St. Louis alone. Construction of new buildings, and renovations of older ones, continued on a daily basis.

In addition to William Lemp's financial success, he was also well liked and popular among the citizens of St. Louis. He was on the boards of several organizations, including a planning committee for the 1904 World's Fair. His family life was happy and his sons were very involved in the business. In November 1892, when the Western Brewery was incorporated as the William J. Lemp Brewing Co., William Jr. was named as vice president and his brother, Louis, was made superintendent.

William Jr., or Billy, as he was commonly known, was born in St. Louis on August 13, 1867. He attended Washington University and the United States Brewer's Academy in New York. He was well known in St. Louis for his flamboyant lifestyle. In 1899 he married Lillian Handlan, the daughter of a wealthy St. Louis manufacturer.

Louis was born on January 11, 1870. He learned the brewer's trade from some of the best master brewers in Germany. He assisted his brother in the management of the company and became involved with several political and civic organizations in St. Louis. As a young man, he had a passion for sports, which he would later turn toward horses, becoming a successful breeder. In 1906, he sold his interest in the brewery and moved to New York to work with horses permanently. He and his wife, Agnes, had one daughter, Louise. Louis died in New York in October 1931.

William's other sons were Frederick, Charles, and Edwin. He also had three daughters: Anna, Elsa, and Hilda. In 1897, Hilda married the son of one of William's best friends, Milwaukee brewer Frederick Pabst. William and Julia also had one other child, a prematurely born infant that died.

During the time of the Lemp Brewery's greatest success, William Lemp purchased a home for his family a short distance away from the brewery complex. The house was built by Jacob Feickert, Julia Lemp's father, in 1868 and was likely financed by William. In 1876, Lemp purchased it outright for use as a residence and as an auxiliary brewery office. Although it was already an impressive house, Lemp immediately began renovating and expanding the mansion and turning it into a showplace of the period. The mansion boasted elegant artwork, handcrafted wood decor, ornately painted ceilings, large, beautiful bathrooms, and even an elevator that replaced the main staircase in 1904. It was a unique and wondrous place and one fitting of the first family of St. Louis brewing.

Ironically, it was in the midst of all of this happiness and success that the Lemp family's troubles began.

The first death in the family was that of Frederick Lemp, William Sr.'s favorite son and the heir apparent to the Lemp empire. He had been groomed for years to take over the family business and was known as the most ambitious and hardworking of the Lemp children. Frederick had been born on November 20, 1873 and attended both Washington University, where he received a degree in mechanical engineering, and the United States Brewers Academy. In 1898, Frederick married Irene Verdin, and the couple was reportedly very happy. Frederick was well known in St. Louis society and was regarded as a friendly and popular fellow. In spite of this, he also spent countless hours at the brewery, working hard to improve the company's future. Some would later say that he worked himself to death.

In 1901, Frederick's health began to fail and he temporarily moved to Pasadena, California, for health reasons. By December, he was much better. William, who had visited his son, returned to St. Louis with hopes that Frederick would be returned to him soon. Unfortunately, that never happened. On December 12, Frederick suffered a sudden relapse and died at the age of twenty-eight. His death was due to heart failure, brought about by complications from other diseases.

Frederick's death was devastating to his parents, especially to his father. Brewery secretary Henry Vahlkamp later wrote that when news came of the young man's death, William Lemp "broke down utterly and cried like a child . . . He took it so seriously that we feared it would completely shatter his health and looked for the worst to happen."

Lemp's friends and coworkers said that he was never the same again after Frederick's death. It was obvious to all of them that he was not coping well and he began to slowly withdraw from the world. He was soon rarely seen in public. Before his son's death, Lemp had taken pleasure in paying the men each week. He also would join the workers in any department and work alongside them in their daily activities or go personally among them and discuss any problems or any questions they had. After Frederick died, though, these practices ceased almost completely.

William slowly recovered from his terrible loss but then, on January 1, 1904, he received the crushing news that his closest friend, Frederick Pabst, had died. William fell apart after this and by February 13, 1904, his suffering had become unbearable.

When William awoke that morning, he ate breakfast and mentioned to one of the servants that he was not feeling well. He finished eating, excused himself, and went back upstairs to his bedroom. Around 9:30, he took a .38-caliber Smith & Wesson revolver and shot himself in the head with it. There was no one else in the house at the time of the shooting except for the servants. A servant girl, upon hearing the sound of the gunshot, ran to the door but she found it locked. She immediately ran to the brewery office, about a half-block away, and summoned Billy and

Edwin. They hurried back to the house and broke down the bedroom door. Inside, they found their father lying on the bed in a pool of blood. The revolver was still gripped in his right hand and there was a gaping, bloody wound at his right temple. At that point, Lemp was still breathing but unconscious.

They called the family physician, Dr. Henry J. Harnisch, by telephone and he came at once. He and three other doctors examined William but there was nothing they could do. William died just as his wife returned home from a shopping trip downtown. No suicide note was ever found.

The Lemp Brewery was very involved in the 1904 World's Fair and Billy took his father's place on the various boards that he was supposed to sit on for the fair. Later that year, he became the new president of the company. Billy was a volatile individual but had a good head for business. Though he spent a fortune on his lavish lifestyle, the company was in its heyday and was making more than enough money to cover his expenses.

In 1899, Billy had married Lillian Handlan, the daughter of a wealthy manufacturer, who had been nicknamed the "Lavender Lady" because of her fondness for wearing that color. They had a stormy marriage and, in 1906, became embroiled in a messy, scandalous divorce trial that had the whole city talking. When it was over, Lillian left St. Louis and Billy went into seclusion at his country estate. In 1915, he married Ellie Limberg, the widow of St. Louis brewer Rudolph Limberg and daughter of Caspar Koehler, president of the Columbia Brewery.

In 1911, the last major improvements were made to the Lemp brewery—giant grain elevators erected on the south side of the complex. With the shadow of Prohibition beginning to fall across the land, Lemp, like many other breweries, began producing a near-beer malt beverage called Cerva. While Cerva did sell moderately well at first, revenues were nowhere near enough to cover the operating expenses used to make it. Eventually, it would be abandoned. It was also in 1911 that the Lemp mansion was converted into the new offices of the brewing company, with private offices and rooms for the clerks.

Business was slow for all German-American brewers through World War I, but the Lemp Brewery fared worse than some of the others. Billy had allowed the company's equipment to deteriorate and had failed to keep abreast of industry innovations, and much of the brewing facilities had become outmoded.

To make matters worse, Prohibition was coming and it would have a devastating effect on all American brewers, including the Lemps. Brewers were stunned by the passing of the amendment and by the Volstead Act, which made prohibition enforceable by law. The more resourceful companies had attempted to market their near-beers, but as alcohol actually became illegal, sales for these inferior brews began to dwindle and then disappear.

This seemed to signal the death of the company. As the individual family members were quite wealthy aside from the profits from the company, there was little incentive to keep the brewery afloat. Billy gave up on the idea that Congress would suddenly repeal Prohibition and he closed the Lemp plant down without notice. The workers learned of the closing when they came to work one day and found the doors shut and the gates locked.

Will decided to simply liquidate the assets of the plant and auction off the buildings. He sold the famous Lemp "Falstaff" logo to brewer Joseph Griesedieck for the sum of $25,000. Griesedieck purchased the recognizable Falstaff name and shield with the idea that eventually the government would see Prohibition for the folly that it was and that beer would be back. Lemp no longer shared the other man's enthusiasm, though, and in 1922, he saw the brewery sold off to the International Shoe Co. for just $588,000, a small fraction of its estimated worth of $7 million in the years before Prohibition.

It was the end of an era for the Lemp family.

Prohibition was only a part of what turned out to be a dismal decade for the Lemp family. It began with the death of Elsa Lemp, the youngest child in the family, born in 1883. After the death of her mother in 1906, she inherited a portion of the Lemp estate and became the wealthiest unmarried woman in the city. In 1910, she became even richer when she married Thomas Wright, the president of the More-Jones Brass and Metal Co. They moved into a home in Hortense Place in St. Louis's Central West End. Their marriage was reportedly an unhappy and stormy one. They separated in December 1918 and in February 1919, Elsa filed for divorce. Unlike her brother's sensational divorce trial, Elsa's legal battle was kept quiet and the details of the divorce were not revealed. It was granted in less than an hour and the reasons were cited as "general indignities."

By March 8, 1920, however, Elsa and Wright had reconciled and the two were remarried in New York City. They returned home to St. Louis and found their house filled with flowers and cards from friends and well-wishers. But all was not happy with the newly remarried couple. Elsa slept little that night, claiming that her stomach was bothering her. When her husband awoke the next morning, Elsa told him that she was feeling better but wanted to remain in bed. Wright agreed that this was the best thing for her and he went into the bathroom and turned on the water in the tub.

He later stated that he heard a loud noise and when he went to see what it was, he found his wife in bed. A pistol lay next to her and she had been shot. No suicide note was ever found and Wright claimed that he had no idea she owned a gun. The only other persons present that morning were members of the household staff. None of them heard the shot, nor did they see any sign that Elsa intended to end her life. The staff quickly summoned Dr. M. B. Clopton and Samuel Fordyce, a family friend. Strangely, the police were not notified of Elsa's death for more than two hours and even then, the news came indirectly through Samuel Fordyce. Wright became "highly agitated" under the scrutiny of the police investigation that followed and his only excuse for not contacting the authorities was that he was bewildered and did not know what to do.

The mysterious circumstances surrounding Elsa's death lead many to believe that there is more to the story than has been told and to this day, some believe that she may have been murdered. That mystery, however, will likely never be solved.

Billy was the next family member to die and his death was also mysterious. He committed suicide, but no clear cause was ever cited. On the morning of December 19, 1922, Lemp secretary Henry Vahlkamp arrived at the Lemp brewery office to find Billy already at his desk. The two of them were joined shortly after by Olivia Bercheck, a stenographer for the brewery and

Billy's personal secretary. Billy had not been feeling well lately and Vahlkamp commented that he looked better.

"You may think so," Billy replied, "but I am feeling worse."

A short time later, while she was downstairs, Olive Bercheck heard a loud noise. When she came upstairs, she found Billy lying on the floor of his office. He had shot himself in the heart with a .38-caliber revolver. When discovered, Lemp was still breathing, but he had expired by the time the doctor arrived. Captain William Doyle, the lead police investigator on the scene, searched Lemp's pockets and desk for a suicide note, but as with his father and his sister before him, Billy left no indication as to why he believed suicide was the answer to his problems.

Oddly, Lemp seemed to have had no intention of suicide, even a short time before. Apparently, the final turn in his downward spiral had come on quite suddenly. After the sale of the brewery, he had discussed selling off the rest of the assets, like land parcels and saloon locations, and planned to then just "take it easy." Not long after that announcement, he had even put his country estate up for sale, stating that he planned to travel to Europe for a while. Even a week before his death, he had dined with his friend August A. Busch, who said that Lemp seemed "cheerful" at the time and that he gave no indication that he was worrying about business or anything else. "He was a fine fellow," Busch added, "and it is hard to believe that he has taken his own life."

With Billy gone and his surviving brothers involved in their own endeavors, it seemed that the days of the Lemp empire had come to an end at last. The two brothers still in St. Louis had left the family enterprise long before it had closed down. Charles worked in banking and finance and Edwin had entered a life of seclusion at his estate in Kirkwood in 1911. The great fortune they had amassed was more than enough to keep the surviving members of the family comfortable through the Great Depression and beyond.

But the days of Lemp tragedy were not yet over.

Disaster continued for the Lemp family. William Lemp III seemed to have inherited his father's troubles with women and went through a nasty divorce in 1936. Three years later he attempted to revive the Lemp name and entered into an agreement with Central Breweries of East St. Louis, Illinois, licensing them to use the Lemp name in connection with their beer. In return, the brewery would pay him royalties on all beer sold with the name of Lemp. In October 1939, Central changed its name to the William J. Lemp Brewing Company and launched a massive advertising campaign to announce the rebirth of the famous Lemp name. Lemp beer began to be officially brewed again on November 1 and initial sales exceeded all expectations. The new endeavor seemed destined for success.

But it barely lasted a year. By September 1940, the William J. Lemp Brewing Company was in serious trouble. They had accumulated a mountain of liabilities and owed back taxes, payrolls, accounts, and interest on second-mortgage bonds. Trading on the company's common stock was suspended on December 19 because the company was deemed insolvent and wiped out. Early the following year, it was officially bankrupt.

The once-strong name of Lemp was now unable to dominate the market as it once had. Ems Brewing Co. took over the brewery in December and they immediately terminated the contract with William Lemp III. Starting on March 1, 1945, they discontinued the name "Lemp" in connection with beer. The plan to bring the Lemp label back to life had failed miserably and the Lemp empire had now breathed its last.

William never lived to see it all fall apart. He suffered a massive brain hemorrhage in December 1943 and died where he was standing.

By the late 1920s, only Charles and Edwin Lemp remained from the immediate family. Throughout his life, Charles was never much involved with the Lemp Brewery, although he was named its treasurer around 1900 and was second vice president in 1911. His interests had been elsewhere. When the family home was renovated into offices, he made his residence at the Racquet Club in St. Louis.

He ended his connections with the family business that same year and took the first of what would be many positions in the banking and financial industries. In 1917, he became vice president of the German Savings Institution and then joined Liberty Central Trust in 1921. He stayed on there for several years and eventually got into the automobile casualty business as president of the Indemnity Company of America. In 1929, Charles moved back into the Lemp mansion and the house became a private residence once more.

He continued to look after his real estate holdings and investments, among which was the East St. Louis, Columbia and Waterloo electric railroad line, which went out of business in 1932. Lemp also enjoyed traveling, which he did extensively until World War II interfered. He was also involved in politics and was a powerful member of the Democratic Party in St. Louis.

Despite his very visible business and political life, Charles remained a mysterious figure who became even odder and more reclusive with age. He remained a bachelor his entire life and lived alone in his old rambling house with only his two servants, Albert and Lena Bittner, for company. By the age of 77, he was quite ill. Legend has it that he was deathly afraid of germs and wore gloves to avoid any contact with bacteria. He was severely arthritic and in almost constant pain. When he could stand it no more, he ended his life.

On May 10, 1949, Alfred Bittner went to the kitchen and prepared breakfast for Charles as he normally did. He then placed the breakfast tray on the desk in the office next to his bedroom. Bittner later recalled that the door to the bedroom was closed and he did not look inside. At about 8:00, Bittner returned to the office to remove the tray and found it untouched. Concerned, he opened the bedroom door to see if Charles was awake and discovered that he was dead from a bullet wound to the head. Bittner hurried to inform his wife of what had happened and she contacted Richard Hawes, Lemp's nephew, who then summoned the police to the mansion.

When the police arrived, they found Charles still in bed and lightly holding a .38-caliber Army Colt revolver in his right hand. He was the only one of the family who had left a suicide note behind. He had dated the letter May 9 and had written "In case I am found dead blame it on no one but me," and had signed it at the bottom.

The Lemp family, which had once been so large and prosperous, had now been almost utterly destroyed in a span of less than a century. Only Edwin Lemp remained. He had long avoided the life that had turned so tragic for the rest of his family. He was known as a quiet, reclusive man who had walked away from the Lemp Brewery in 1913 to live a peaceful life on his secluded estate in Kirkwood. Here, he communed with nature and became an excellent cook, gourmet, and animal lover. He collected fine art and entertained his intimate friends.

Edwin managed to escape from the family "curse," but as he grew older, he did become more eccentric and developed a terrible fear of being alone. He never spoke about his family or their tragic lives, but they must have preyed on him all the same. His fears caused him to simply entertain more and to keep a companion with him at his estate almost all the time. Edwin passed away quietly of natural causes at age ninety in 1970.

After the death of Charles Lemp, the family mansion was sold and turned into a boardinghouse. Shortly after that, it fell on hard times and began to deteriorate, along with the surrounding neighborhood. In later years, stories began to emerge that residents of the boardinghouse often complained of ghostly knocks and phantom footsteps in the house. As these tales spread, it became increasingly hard to find tenants to occupy the rooms and because of this, the old Lemp Mansion was rarely filled.

The house's decline continued until 1975, when Richard Pointer and his family purchased it. The Pointers began remodeling and renovating the place, working for many years to turn it into a combination restaurant and inn. But they were soon to find out that they were not alone in the house. Construction workers reported that ghostly events were occurring in the house as they worked to remodel it. Almost all of them confessed that they believed the place was haunted and told of feeling as though they were being watched. They spoke of hearing unexplained sounds and complained of tools that vanished and then returned in different places from where they had been left.

At one point in the renovations, a painter was brought in to work on the ceilings. He stayed in the house overnight while he completed the job. One day, he ran downstairs to tell one of the Pointers that he had heard the sound of horses' hooves on the cobblestones outside his window. Pointer convinced the painter that he was mistaken; there were no horses and no cobblestones

outside the house. In time, the man finished the ceilings and left, but the story stayed on Pointer's mind. Later that year, he noticed that some of the grass in the yard had turned brown. He dug it up and found that beneath the top level of soil was a layer of cobblestones. During the Lemps' residency in the house, that portion of the yard had been a drive leading to the carriage house.

Later in the restoration, another artist was brought in to restore the painted ceiling in one of the front dining rooms. It had been covered over with paper years before. While he was lying on his back on the scaffolding, the artist felt a sensation that he believed was a "spirit" moving past him. It frightened him so badly that he left the house without his brushes and tools and refused to return and get them. A few months after this event, an elderly man came into the restaurant and told one of the staff members that he had once been a driver for the Lemp family. He explained that the ceiling in the dining room had been papered over because William Lemp hated the design that had been painted on it. The staff members, upon hearing this story, recalled the artist saying that he had gotten the distinct impression that the "spirit" he encountered had been angry. Was it perhaps because he was restoring the unwanted ceiling painting?

During the restorations, the Pointers' son, Dick, lived alone in the house and became quite an expert on the ghostly manifestations. One night, he was lying in bed reading when he heard a door slam loudly in another part of the house. No one else was supposed to be there and he was sure that he had locked all of the doors. Fearing that someone might have broken in, he and his dog, a Doberman pinscher named Shadow, decided to take a look around. The dog was spooked by this time, having also heard the sound, and she had her ears turned up, listening for anything else. They searched the entire house and found no one there. Every door was locked, just as Pointer had left them. He reported that the same thing happened again about a month later; again, no sign of an intruder was found.

After the restaurant opened, staff members began to report their own odd experiences. Glasses were seen to lift off the bar and fly through the air, sounds were often heard that had no explanation, and some people even glimpsed apparitions that appeared and vanished. In addition, many customers and visitors to the house reported some pretty weird incidents. It was said that doors locked and unlocked themselves on their own, the piano in the bar played by itself, voices and sounds came from nowhere, and the ghost of a woman was seen occasionally. Some claimed that it was Lillian Handlan, Billy's ex-wife and the famed "Lavender Lady," even though she never actually lived in the house. Perhaps the indignities that she suffered at the hands of her former husband managed to draw her to his family's home after death.

While the ghostly atmosphere of the place has admittedly attracted a number of curious patrons, it has also caused the Pointers to lose a number of valuable employees. One of them was a former waitress named Bonnie Strayhorn, who encountered an unusual customer while working one day. The restaurant had not yet opened for business when she saw a dark-haired man seated at one of the tables in the rear dining room. She was surprised that someone had come in so early, but she went over to ask if he would like a cup of coffee. He simply sat unmoving and did not answer. Bonnie frowned and glanced away for a moment. When she looked back moments later, the man was gone. She has continued to maintain that he could not have left the room in the brief seconds when she was not looking at him. After that incident, Bonnie left the Lemp Mansion and went to work in a non-haunted location.

The house has attracted ghost hunters from across the country. Many of them are lured by the publicity the house has received as a haunted location. The mansion has appeared in scores of magazines, newspaper articles, books, and television shows over the years, first gaining national attention in November 1980 when *Life* magazine included it in an article entitled "Terrifying Tales of Nine Haunted Houses."

As the years have passed, the Lemp Mansion has continued to lure visitors who are looking for strange and ghostly happenings and I have stayed the night here many times myself. As Paul Pointer once said, those who come to this house are rarely disappointed and I would have to agree. While not all of my stays at this old house have been eventful ones, at least when it comes to ghosts, I have to say that the vivid sense of history that I have experienced when I'm here more than makes up for the lack of anything supernatural. If you're a ghost hunter, or a history buff, then I encourage you to visit the mansion of the once-mighty Lemp family. Their empire may have crumbled long ago but there is much to see here among the ruins of yesteryear.

McDowell Medical College

St. Louis is considered today to be one of the outstanding medical training centers in the United States. Over the years, dozens of medical schools have flourished in the city, along with many excellent hospitals, but not since Dr. Joseph McDowell's college was closed just before the Civil War has there been another school like his. It was a place rife with wild rumors, lurid stories, and tales of the owner's eccentricities.

And unfortunately, most of those stories were true.

The McDowell Medical College was founded in 1840 as the Medical Department of Kemper College. It became the first medical school established west of the Mississippi. The head of the medical school was Dr. Joseph McDowell. McDowell's school remained connected with Kemper College until 1847, when financial problems forced Kemper to drop the program. At that point, McDowell struck out on his own and constructed a building to house the school at Ninth and Gratiot Streets. It became one of the most notorious buildings in the city and later would even become a Confederate prison during the Civil War.

The infamy of the building was often overshadowed by the notoriety of the school's founder. Joseph McDowell was considered to be one of the finest doctors of his day. His eccentricities aside, he was thought of as an excellent physician and a very capable surgeon in a city where medical standards were high. Many graduates of other medical schools in St. Louis would attend lectures at the McDowell school as part of a graduate course. McDowell came from a distinguished medical family; his uncle, Ephraim McDowell, was the first doctor to successfully perform an ovariotomy (a surgical incision into an ovary).

In spite of this, it was McDowell's personality traits that got him talked about in the city. He was described as having "an erratic temperament that approached insanity" and he was often said to be horribly jealous and suspicious of other doctors and schools. He was also an ardent secessionist and believed strongly in the rights of the southern states and in the institution of slavery. To make his volatile political positions quite clear, he often placed a loaded revolver on the table in front of him when discussing issues of slavery, states' rights, or secession. While known for being generous in his treatment of the poor, he was also known for his hatred of immigrants, African Americans, and Catholics. He would lecture on those subjects at street corners to anyone who would listen. After receiving numerous death threats, he started to wear a breastplate of armor on a regular basis.

The building on Gratiot Street reflected McDowell's eccentricities. McDowell had invested $150,000 of his own money into the school and it became the largest building devoted exclusively to medicine in the United States. It was designed with two large wings and was flanked by an octagonal tower. The tower had been fitted with an unusual deck around which six cannons had been placed to defend the school against possible attack. He also kept the school stocked with muskets that could be handed out to the students during a potential attack. During patriotic holidays, McDowell would pass out the rifles and march the students into the field along Seventh Street. After a short speech, he would give the command to fire off the guns and to set off the cannons in the direction of Mill Creek. The staff and students at the Christian Brothers College next door always beat a hasty retreat when they saw the medical students assembling on the lawn.

The building had other unusual elements as well. The central column of the tower had niches that were intended to hold the remains of the McDowell family members after their deaths. The bodies were to be placed in alcohol-filled copper tubes. The building also included a dissecting room, a chemical room, a lecture hall, a laboratory, and a dispensary where the poor were treated for free. There was also a rooftop observatory and offices for the doctors on staff. A massive anatomical amphitheater was fitted with six large windows so that dissections could be done under natural light. McDowell also opened a museum that contained more than three thousand specimens of North American wildlife. There were also minerals, fossils, and antiquities, all of which could be viewed for a 25-cent admission. The clergy and medical men were admitted for free. While the building was equipped with all of the latest medical facilities, there were no living quarters at the school; students were expected to live in the boardinghouses of the neighborhood.

McDowell was especially known for his surgical skills and he emphasized anatomy in his classes. As part of their coursework, the students had to take part in human dissection—a practice that would bring notoriety to the school and the building. In those days, it was nearly impossible for medical colleges to get bodies for research, because dissection was against the law. To obtain bodies for study, McDowell was forced to introduce the art of "body snatching" to St. Louis, although he preferred to refer to his and his students' nighttime forays into the city's cemeteries as "resurrectionist activities."

No matter what McDowell called it, local residents were horrified when they discovered just what was going on behind the walls of the college—and where the fresh cadavers were coming from. For the most part, the school was superstitiously avoided as a haunted place, but occasionally, the more courageous citizens could be stirred into mob action. The disappearance of a German immigrant woman started a riot at McDowell College when rumors spread that she had been killed and turned into a medical specimen. Everyone knew that McDowell hated immigrants, so he was quickly regarded as a suspect. The woman was later found, however, wandering the streets of Alton, Illinois, in a demented state.

It would be an incident involving one of McDowell's stolen corpses that would change his entire attitude about the possibility of ghosts and life after death. At one time, McDowell was an outspoken critic of anyone who believed in ghosts or other "such frauds without foundation," but that was before the spirit of his dead mother apparently saved his life.

A German girl who lived in the neighborhood died of an unusual disease and McDowell and some of his students stole her body and hid it away in one of the laboratories. News spread of the theft and many of the local Germans became angry and vowed to break into the school and find the body.

"I received a note at my house," Dr. McDowell later wrote, "warning me that the visit was to be that night." Quickly, the doctor went down to the college to hide the body. When he arrived all was quiet and he went into the dissecting room with a light. He lifted the girl's corpse onto his shoulder, planning to carry it to the attic and conceal it in the rafters, or perhaps to hide it in a cedar chest that was out of sight in one of the closets.

"I had ascended one flight of stairs," he continued, "when out went my lamp. I laid down the corpse, and re-struck the light. I then picked up the body, when out went my light again. I felt for another match in my pocket, when I saw distinctly my dear, dead mother, standing a little distance off, beckoning to me."

McDowell said that he saw her rise up a little in front of a window and then vanish. Shaken, he walked close to the wall and climbed to the attic, where he hid the body away. He came back downstairs in the darkness and when he reached the window, he saw two Germans talking. One of them had a shotgun and the other carried a revolver. The doctor slipped quietly down the staircase and when he got to the door of the dissecting room, he looked down the stairs into the hallway below. There were another five or six men there, one of whom was lighting a lamp.

"I hesitated a moment as to what I should do," wrote McDowell, "as I had left my pistols in the room where I took the body. I looked in the room, as it was my only chance to get away, when I saw my spirit mother standing near the table from which I had taken the corpse. I had no light, but the halo that surrounded my mother was sufficient to enable me to see the table quite plainly."

Suddenly, footsteps sounded on the staircase below and McDowell darted into the dissection room. He lay down on the table where the girl's body had been and pulled a sheet up over his face. The men came into the room to look for the dead girl among the other bodies that had been placed there. Sheets were lifted from the faces of the corpses and when they passed the table where McDowell was hiding, one of them commented on the freshness of the corpse and that he had died with his boots on. However, they did not look under the sheet. McDowell was terrified that he would be discovered but claimed that he heard a soft voice in his ear, urging him to be still.

The Germans searched the building, but they never stumbled onto the body of the girl and did not discover they were not alone in the college. Finally, McDowell heard their boots stomping down the steps and outside. Somehow, he had been saved.

The Civil War ushered in a new, equally gruesome chapter in the history of the Gratiot Street building. When the war began, McDowell's son, Drake, joined the Confederate Army under the command of Gen. Meriwether Jeff Thompson. He took two of the school's cannons with him. McDowell had already shipped the 1,400 muskets that he had collected to the South in boxes labeled "polished marble." After that, he also went south to serve the Confederacy as medical director for the Trans-Mississippi Department.

In November 1861, Gen. Henry Halleck took over as commander of the Union Army's Department of the West, headquartered in St. Louis. He converted the McDowell Medical School into a prison for captured Confederate soldiers.

The first captives arrived at the Gratiot Street Prison on December 22. It was soon obvious that the prison had been poorly planned and prepared. The building's capacity was about one-third of the number of prisoners that arrived on the first day. The holding areas were badly ventilated and not suited for large numbers of people, and the latrine procedures that were planned quickly became useless.

Conditions were chaotic because of the lack of organization. Prisoners of all types could be housed in the same rooms. Held within the walls were not only Confederate prisoners of war, but suspected Southern sympathizers, bushwhackers, spies, Union deserters, Union soldiers arrested for criminal activity, and, separated from the rest of the prisoners, women accused of harboring fugitives or sympathizing with the South.

Discipline in the prison was harsh, especially in the beginning when St. Louis was still embroiled in the unrest, riots, murders, and shootings that marked the early days of the war. Guards were ordered to shoot not only anyone who tried to escape, but even anyone who simply stuck a head or body part out of a window. And the guards were often accused of showing no hesitancy to shoot. It was said that they often took potshots at the prisoners just to practice their aim.

The prison was a filthy, horrifying place. The population soared and sanitary conditions and food rations declined further. The hospital was always full, so the sick and dying were left lying on the floor among the other prisoners. The dawn of each new day would reveal from one to four dead men stretched out on the cold stone. One prisoner wrote, "All through the night can be heard coughing, swearing, singing and praying, sometimes drowned out by almost unearthly noises, issuing from uproarious gangs, laughing, shouting, stamping and howling, making night hideous with their unnatural clang. It is surely a hell on earth."

The lack of space, the poor food, and the lack of medical care plagued the prison. In March 1863, a smallpox epidemic raged through the close quarters and the polluted conditions in the lower rooms declined further. Lice and bedbugs invaded the prisoners, their clothing, and everything else. Prisoners died at an alarming rate, largely due to new outbreaks of smallpox and typhoid.

A constant stream of new inmates, many of whom were dead on arrival or died soon after, propelled the population at Gratiot Street to new highs in 1864. Horrified at the rate of death and illness within the prison walls, Union Surgeon General George Rex reported that despite the attention that had been called to the problem of overcrowding, the "evil still continues unabated." The prison remained open until the end of the war. By then, the conditions inside had collapsed beyond imagination.

McDowell survived the war, and after traveling and lecturing in Europe, returned to St. Louis. In the summer of 1865, he reestablished the medical school. He cleaned and renovated all of the rooms, except for one, which was left just as it had been when the prison was open. He called that room "Hell" and, most likely, the description was a fitting one.

McDowell died in 1868 and the medical school was left vacant for years. In June 1878, the south wing was condemned as being unsafe and was demolished by order of the fire department. The octagonal tower and the north wing remained until 1882, when they were torn down. Nothing remains of the building today and it is merely a forgotten spot on the Ralston-Purina lot.

But for years after the building closed down for good, it was anything but a forgotten place for the people who lived in the neighborhood around the old college. To them it was a "haunted" and forbidding place, and not only because of the horrific experiments they believed had been conducted by Dr. McDowell and his students. The people in the area were convinced that the ghosts of men who died at the Gratiot Street Prison remained behind at the site.

According to the stories, cries and screams were often heard coming from the crumbling walls of the old prison. If anyone searched the building after hearing these screams, they would find the place empty and abandoned. What could they have been hearing? Could it have been an eerie replay of the cacophony that was described by prisoners during the war? One of the prisoners wrote that on many nights, it was impossible to sleep because of the sounds that came from the lower levels of the prison. The natural sounds of incarcerated men were "sometimes drowned out by almost unearthly noises . . . laughing, shouting, stamping and howling, making night hideous with their unnatural clang."

Could this have been the sound described by the terrified local residents as the horror of yesterday continued into the present?

Jefferson Barracks

Military officers and soldiers have been with St. Louis since the very beginnings of the city. Soldiers were among the first to arrive in the city, though no actual military post was ever constructed under French or Spanish rule. It was not until the Americans took over the city in 1804 that an actual garrison was established. Fort Bellefountaine was built in 1805 to protect the pioneers and settlers who were heading west to the frontier. At that time, the fort, located just north of St. Louis near the confluence of the Mississippi and Missouri Rivers, was the most remote post built by the Army. It would provide crucial military protection to St. Louis and the region's fur trade for the next twenty years.

By 1826, however, Fort Bellefountaine had fallen into deplorable condition. The buildings were dilapidated and the whole place was considered "unhealthy," thanks to frequent flooding. It was finally decided that the site should be abandoned. On March 4, 1826, Col. Henry Atkinson was assigned to find a more suitable location for a new military post in St. Louis.

The site that Atkinson selected was south of the city. The spot was in a fine natural position and there was an abundance of natural building supplies, as well as a nearby civilian population from which both supplies and labor could be obtained. The new post was dubbed Jefferson Barracks and it was officially established on October 23, 1826. The fort was named in honor of former president Thomas Jefferson, who had died earlier that same year.

The earliest role of Jefferson Barracks was to house the soldiers who protected the settlers from Indian attacks. In April 1832, a steamship of troops were sent north to participate in the Black Hawk War. A young lieutenant named Jefferson Davis, who would later go on to serve as the president of the Confederacy during the Civil War, was assigned to escort the captured Indian leader back to Jefferson Barracks. In 1836, other troops from the post would be sent to Florida to take part in battles against the Seminole Indians.

Life at the frontier post was difficult in the early days. Lt. Philip St. George Cooke, who graduated from West Point in 1827 and came to Jefferson Barracks on his first assignment in what would be a long and distinguished military career, had little good to say about the conditions of the fort. He recalled the infantrymen being crowded several to a room in stone barracks that were half-finished and uncomfortable. During the summer, the heat in the region was oppressive and the flooded marshes along the Mississippi River bred insects and diseases, including cholera, yellow fever, and smallpox.

A soldier's military training at that time consisted mostly of small-arms practice on the parade field, marching, and guard duty. For the most part, life in the garrison was boring and monotonous and when left to their own devices, the men usually turned to drinking, fighting, and visiting the local prostitutes. This led to harsh disciplinary measures. The most common offenses perpetrated by enlisted men were drunkenness and desertion. In most case, soldiers found guilty of drinking were reduced in rank and fined. Other punishments included being abused, threatened, and even beaten. Deserters who had been captured were incarcerated in the post's stockade, where they were subjected to harsh and sadistic punishment, in addition to living in cramped and foul cells that were infested with bedbugs. Prisoners were sometimes hanged by their thumbs or shackled to the floor with chains. It's not surprising that to this day, at least one of the old stockades is allegedly inhabited by soldiers still seeking release. It was torn down years ago but occupants of the building constructed on the site have often reported apparitions of uniformed men who wander about aimlessly, as though trapped in place. They are believed to be ghost of prisoners, still incarcerated here, at least in spirit.

Jefferson Barracks was first used as staging area for troops and equipment in 1846, during the Mexican War. When the fighting ended, the post was also used as a "mustering out" point for men returning to civilian life. This would take place again during many wars to follow, including the Civil War, when the post would play an important role in St. Louis. The state of Missouri was sharply divided between North and South, but Jefferson Barracks and the Federal Arsenal in St. Louis remained loyal to the Federal government.

When war was declared in April 1861, Jefferson Barracks became a training post for Missouri's Union volunteers. Men and equipment poured into the post, arriving and departing by land, rail, and river steamer. The roads to Jefferson Barracks were inundated with militia, horses, artillery, and regular Army units. To complicate matters, thousands of volunteers for the Union flooded the post as well.

As the war entered its second year, Jefferson Barracks changed from an armed camp to a Federal medical facility. In the fall of 1862, the Army Medical Department built nine temporary medical buildings on the post. Injured troops were transported to the barracks by train and boat from all over the country. Most hospitals during the war were terrifying and unsanitary places, Jefferson Barracks included. The facilities were overcrowded and dirty and ignorance and disease killed more men than battle wounds did.

Medical procedures slowly began to improve, but while the facilities at Jefferson Barracks were reportedly better than most, there were still cases of men who were injured or permanently crippled by the carelessness of post physicians. Not surprisingly, the hospitals of Jefferson Barracks have their own ghostly stories to tell.

After the Civil War, Jefferson Barracks continued providing troops and support for the Indian wars in the West. The post would see action again in 1898 when America became embroiled in the Spanish-American War in Cuba. Once again, Jefferson Barracks served as an induction point and training center for volunteers and National Guardsmen who were called up to serve. The war ended in August 1898 and victorious troops arrived at Jefferson Barracks from Cuba, Puerto Rico, and Manila to be mustered out of the service.

In 1915, Jefferson Barracks also took part in a military campaign that is largely forgotten today. This operation was under the command of Gen. John "Black Jack" Pershing and it was organized to capture the Mexican bandit leader Pancho Villa, who had been conducting raids into American territory.

But there was another conflict that officers at Jefferson Barracks were watching more closely, a conflict that was threatening to become the "war to end all wars." Battles were raging across Europe, while America waited and watched. Beginning in 1914, German planes and airships starting bombing England and France and their submarines were sending ships to the bottom of the ocean. Finally, attacks on merchant vessels sailing to and from the United States drew America into the war and a formal declaration against Germany was made on April 6, 1917.

Jefferson Barracks was again to serve as the country's leading induction site and thousands of soldiers passed through the post on their way to the battlefields of Europe. By 1919, it was all over and the soldiers returned to St. Louis and back to civilian life.

In January 1922, President Warren G. Harding ordered a section of Jefferson Barracks to become the home of a Veterans Hospital, which opened in March 1923. The physicians were given the task of caring for wounded and invalid soldiers and the hospital began providing continuous treatment for veterans until the base closed down. During the years of its operation, the building became known for hosting a ghost.

According to one story, a private Halloween party was held at the hospital one year. Security officers who worked the gate later commented to one of the party organizers about the "excellent" Civil War officer's uniform that one of the guests had worn to the party. The official was taken aback and replied that there had been no one wearing such a costume. The security officer was just as surprised because he distinctly remembered a man in a Civil War-era uniform who had entered the hospital grounds, presumably to attend the party that was going on.

Jefferson Barracks was back in the action again at the start of World War II. In the days and weeks after the 1941 attack on Pearl Harbor, thousands of soldiers passed through Jefferson Barracks on their way to military service. During the course of the war, it is estimated that more than 400,000 soldiers were processed and trained at the post.

Jefferson Barracks was also used as a prisoner-of-war camp during World War II. More than four hundred German and Italian soldiers were confined to the base; during the Flood of 1943, the prisoners helped to fill sandbags and worked side by side with their captors to hold back the river. The prisoners were regularly used as laborers on the base, except for a short time in 1945, when they participated in a work strike to protest the treatment of a prisoner. They laid down their tools and refused to work, but eventually a diet of only bread and water brought them peacefully back to their labors.

With the end of the war came the end of Jefferson Barracks. On June 30, 1946, the post's flag was lowered for the final time. Of the original 1,700 acres, the Missouri Air National Guard acquired 135 acres and the rest was deemed to be "surplus." In the years that followed, the property fell into a state of decay and vandals and souvenir hunters managed to damage the old and unattended buildings. In 1950, however, the St. Louis County Parks and Recreation Department acquired 500 acres of the land to create the Jefferson Barracks Historical Park. Today, it holds athletic fields, picnic shelters, an amphitheater, and several museums.

The military has not altogether abandoned the site either. These days, it is home to units of the Missouri Air National Guard, the Missouri Army National Guard, and the U.S. Army Reserve. There are forty-one buildings remaining on the post and both military and civilian employees occupy thirty-five of them at different times. The buildings serve as administrative offices, classrooms, and maintenance facilities for the National Guard and reserve units on the base, while others serve as storage areas and warehouses.

And out of these dozens of historic buildings, a great many are haunted!

Many of the ghost stories told at Jefferson Barracks have been a part of the local lore for years. Some of them even date back as far as the Civil War. One such tale is that of the specter who has been reported on the grounds near the post headquarters.

During the Civil War, and for years afterward, soldiers guarded the train depot and the railroad tracks located along the Mississippi River. They also guarded the headquarters building that was located on the bluff above the depot. One night during the Civil War, a sentry was walking his beat near the building. As he rounded the corner, he observed a solitary figure walking up the grassy hill from the train yard. As the soldier stood watching, he realized that the man was not a person at all, but what he described as a blurry "spook."

There is also a long-running legend about a ghost who haunts the post's old powder magazine. The massive limestone building was built in 1857 as a secure location to store rifles, cannons, and gunpowder for the troops at the post. In 1871, the Federal Arsenal in St. Louis was closed and its contents were also moved to Jefferson Barracks. The powder magazine remained in constant use until the post closed in 1946. In more recent times, it has become a historical museum that is run by the St. Louis County Parks and Recreation Department.

The story of the ghost here has its beginnings around the start of World War II. In the dark days at the start of the war, sentries were posted all around the fort to protect it from possible incursion. One of the most important guard positions was the powder magazine. Armed sentries were often seen patrolling around the building or walking across the top of the stone wall that surrounded the magazine. Several of the soldiers who stood guard here reported seeing a ghostly sentry who would occasionally appear and challenge the confused guard who was standing his post. The threatening spirit was said to have "a bullet hole in his head, running red with blood" and was said to be so frightening that several guards allegedly threw down their guns and deserted their posts after encountering him. One story had it that a certain soldier was so frightened that he not only left his post one night, but that he also left the army!

According to the story, the spectral sentry was a guard who had been killed years before when a raiding party attempted to steal munitions from the powder magazine. He was believed to have confronted his living counterparts because he thought they were trespassers. Even after all of these years, he was still on duty, even in death.

Another old story tells of a ghost who long haunted the grounds around the post's old north gate. He is believed to be the spirit of 2nd Lt. Thomas May, who was killed in a duel near the north gate in 1830. There are also legends of a ghostly woman who has been spotted at the Laborer's House, a historic structure that was built in 1851. It was once used as a residence by civilians who worked at the ordnance depot and today is operated as a gift shop by the Parks Department.

The Post Headquarters, or Building 1, was constructed in 1900. Built on the edge of the parade field and on a bluff overlooking the river, the three-story brick building has seen many occupants over the years. The most famous ghost to haunt this building is believed to be the spirit of a Civil War general, and has been seen in the post commander's office. A number of employees have reported seeing a shadowy figure, seated at a desk near a window on the second floor of the building. The apparition appears to be writing dispatches by candlelight and has the hazy outlines of a man in uniform. When employees enter the building and attempt to investigate the second-floor office, though, the figure has always vanished. Strangely, they have discovered that when they approach the doorway to the room, they often hear the sound of footsteps walking away from them. However, there is no other way out of the room and no one inside of it.

Building 28 was built in 1897 as a double barracks with a three-story tower in the center. It had been designed to house up to four companies of cavalry soldiers and their non-commissioned officers. Throughout the years, men working inside of the building have reported hearing ghostly footsteps pacing the corridors and talked of lights that turned on and off without assistance.

Building 78, which is also known as Atkinson Hall, was erected in 1912 to serve as the post's main dining facility. The structure, with its distinctive whitewashed exterior, was planned to replace the old dining hall, which had been dubbed the "Cockroach Bogey." The building was always extremely busy during "chow time" and served as a focal point of activity for the soldiers here until the post closed down in 1946.

Years after the post closed, the building was renovated for the new occupants of the site, the Army Reserve and the National Guard. During these renovations, one of the greatest mysteries of the building was uncovered. While work was being done, a secret room was discovered on the third floor, near the main staircase. The room was not shown on any of the building plans and had obviously been added without anyone's knowledge. Inside of the room, workers found a collection of military personnel files, books, and photographs from the early part of the century. The mystery of this room was compounded by the story that the contractor who had designed the building also committed suicide inside of it a few years later. Could his ghost be one of the phantoms who have been reported wandering the hallways?

Today, Building 78 is used by several units from the Missouri National Guard and apparently plays host to a variety of spirits. Several military and civilian employees have reported that the ghost of a World War I–era soldier walks through the building, apparently looking around and ensuring that everything is secure. Others have reported phantom footsteps, shadowy apparitions, and weird cold spots that appear without explanation.

Another haunted location, the Jefferson Barracks "Station" Hospital, was built around 1905 and served the soldiers of the post until the base was closed down in 1946. The third floor of the brick building served as a surgical center, while the basement housed the morgue. When Jefferson Barracks was closed and many of the outer buildings of the post were sold off to companies and individuals, the hospital became the property of the Mehlville School District.

The hospital served as a high school for a number of years but today it is used as the school district's facilities department. It is mainly used for storage; few people spend much time in the building anymore, but there have been a number of employees here over the years. Those who have been in the building after hours report the sounds of ghostly footsteps roaming the hallways and incidents where lights have turned on and off by themselves. There is also the ghost of a child who has been seen walking through the basement. She always vanishes without explanation.

One could argue that, based on its size, Jefferson Barracks is the most haunted location in the St. Louis area. There are scores of ghosts and hauntings at this historic spot, many of them still waiting to be unearthed.

West of the City

Ghosts of St. Charles

The South Main Street antique district in St. Charles is a quaint, historic area with a number of original buildings and a distinguished past. This small town, built alongside the Missouri River, dates back more than two centuries, and the footsteps of history have certainly left their mark on the brick streets and cobblestone walks. This may be one of the reasons why the town is considered so haunted and why South Main Street has so many ghosts. But it's not only the passage of time that has left spirits behind— some believe an old cemetery may have something to do with it too.

The first settlers came to St. Charles in 1769 when a French-Canadian trapper named Louis Blanchette arrived in the area. He started a small settlement and called the region *Les Petites Cotes* or "The Little Hills." Blanchette became the first commander of St. Charles, under Spanish rule, but the area was soon filled with French settlers. In 1800, Spain gave the Louisiana Territory to France; in 1804, it was sold to the United States. President Thomas Jefferson then ordered an expedition to explore the new region and to chart the course of the Missouri River. Jefferson put the command of the expedition into the hands of Meriwether Lewis and William Clark. In May 1804, the two men gathered supplies for their journey in St. Charles before departing for the western frontier.

Another famous explorer connected to St. Charles was Daniel Boone, who arrived from Kentucky in 1795. He joined his sons, who had a homestead south of town. Boone continued to explore the region and a trail that he created here, Boone's Lick Road, became the starting point for both the Oregon and Santa Fe Trails. Boone's home is located near St. Charles and it has been said that the ghost of his wife, Rebecca, can still be found lingering near her gravesite there.

As St. Charles began to grow, it saw an influx of German settlers, thanks to reports that the area resembled the Rhine Valley back in Germany. German businesses began to spring up all over town, including a tobacco factory and a brewery. In 1821, when Missouri became a state, its first capital was St. Charles. The capital remained there for five years while a permanent building was constructed in Jefferson City.

The history of the town seems to lend itself to ghosts, and nowhere is this as evident as along the historic Main Street, which lies along the river. This brick-paved roadway is unrivaled by any in the area for its collection of craft and antique shops and, of course, for the myriad hauntings that plague the area.

Many believe that it's not just history that has been left behind. They blame the hauntings on the old St. Borromeo Cemetery, which was established in 1789 in the 400 block of what is now South Main Street. Although the bodies were exhumed and moved to a newer graveyard on Randolph Street in the 1800s, it's rumored that a number of bodies were left behind.

John Dengler, who owned the reportedly haunted Farmer's Home Building and opened a shop there in 1917, was convinced that many of the bodies buried in the old cemetery were never found. He distinctly recalled some work that was done behind a corner building that is sometimes called the Armory or the French Armory. A construction crew, excavating to enlarge a nearby structure, dug into the hillside and found a large number of bodies that had not been removed. At another site, a cluster of forgotten bones was encased in concrete when the floor of the building was laid.

Dengler often stated that every building on South Main Street had a story to tell, and in some places, the ghost stories were the greatest stories of all. The Farmer's Home Building, where he owned a tobacco shop, was one such place. The building was constructed on the old cemetery site around 1815 and up until 1856, it was the Farmer's Tavern, a popular hotel and restaurant. Dengler's shop was located in what was once the ladies' dining room of the inn and sometimes the smell of ham and green beans wafts through the air, even though no one is cooking.

It was not uncommon for people to hear footsteps on the stairs and in the hallways of the building. Voices were often heard, usually speaking French. During one memorable "ghost outbreak," the French-speaking apparition seemed to delight in playing tricks, often making cigarette packs float through the air or turn up in odd places. The radio often switched from talk shows to music without the dial ever moving. One day, a crying baby was heard, following by the soothing voice of someone speaking French.

Who were the ghosts of the Farmer's Home building? John Dengler never knew whether they were former guests of the hotel or spirits of those left behind in the St. Borromeo Cemetery. But they were welcome to stay, he often said, as long as they behaved themselves.

Another haunting on South Main Street is a restaurant known as the Mother-in-Law House. The house was built in 1866 by Francis Kremer, the owner of a flourishing mill in the city. It is believed to be the first double house built in St. Charles. Around the time of its construction, the house earned its rather peculiar nickname, which it still enjoys today. It seems that Mrs. Kremer was very homesick for her mother, so her husband built the house with both sides exactly alike. Once side was for the family and the other side was for Kremer's mother-in-law. The building today is a restaurant that plays host to hungry customers—and to an unearthly spirit.

Owner Donna Hafer long spoke of the fact that nothing ever seemed to go right on the northern side of the restaurant—the side that was once occupied by Francis Kremer's mother-in-law. Over the years, many customers have spoken of the strange events, including glasses, drinks, and utensils that disappear with no explanation; water glasses that mysteriously spill; coffee cups that upend and dump their contents in the laps of guests; food that inexplicably changes temperature; and more.

Eventually, Donna decided to redecorate that end of the building. While the ghost remained behind, she no longer seemed unhappy about being there.

According to reports, the Boone's Lick Trail Inn also had a resident ghost. The owners stated that this spirit was actually very helpful, though, assisting them as they climbed a certain flight of stairs, which are narrow and uneven. A previous owner of the place had warned them about other activity, but for years, a well-placed hand to steady them on the staircase was the only sign of a presence. Some have suggested that this ghost may be the spirit of a former occupant who met his or her own death on these stairs.

The David McNair House at 724 South Main was long home to a "cooking ghost." Occupants reported over the years that at the oddest times, the house suddenly filled with the smell of home-cooked soup, even though nothing was cooking there at all.

The historic Winery of the Little Hills was allegedly home to two separate ghosts. Witnesses stated that the apparitions were a man and a woman in period clothing who vanished whenever they were approached. They may not have been the only ghosts that haunted the place either. Apparently, there were also mischievous spirits who would steal silverware, only to return it later in unusual places. They were also said to wreak havoc in the bar area, spilling wine, rearranging glasses, and moving things around.

The ghost of a little girl has been reported in a number of different buildings along South Main Street, including in 523 and 519 South Main. The stories say that she is the ghost of a child who died after being badly burned around a stove in the 1940s, but no one really knows for sure. A former employee of a shop at 523 used to talk of seeing the little girl quite often. While working, the employee would sometimes see metal racks sway and spin by themselves. Whenever she spoke up and asked the little girl to stop, she always did. There was also a miniature sewing machine in the store that the little ghost girl liked to play with. The employees would always put it away at night but when they came in the next day, they would often find it out on the counter or in another part of the store.

One of the most famous haunted universities in the St. Louis region is Lindenwood College, located in St. Charles. The college was founded in 1827 by Mary Easton Sibley, the daughter of St. Louis's first postmaster and the original founder of the city of Alton, Illinois, Col. Rufus Easton. Married at the age of only fifteen to Maj. George Sibley, Mary never had any children of her own. Her husband was a military surveyor for the Santa Fe Trail who began his career in western Missouri at Fort Osage. In 1825, he was chosen to lead an expedition along the Santa Fe Trail and managed to bring national attention to it. Sibley, a longtime Indian agent, also negotiated a successful treaty with the Osage Indians, who agreed to give safe passage to settlers along the trail in exchange for $800.

After his work for the military was completed, Sibley and his wife settled in St. Charles. By that time, Mary had already started taking in students. Not long after, Major Sibley was given a parcel of land as payment on a bad debt. On the land was a large hill that Mary decided to use to build a school; the hill, covered with linden trees, was called Lindenwood, and the college took on this name. The school soon opened in a large log cabin and became the first university for women west of the Mississippi River.

The school prospered and Mary remained devoted to it throughout her life. In fact, legend has even stated that Mary's ghost is said to be responsible for the good luck that has come to the school; before her death, Mary reportedly promised the students that she would always watch over them. Her body remains behind as well. She is buried with her family in a small cemetery on the campus.

Not surprisingly, the most famous haunted spot on campus is Sibley Hall. This was the former Sibley family home and it later became the school's first residence hall. Back in the days when it was being used as a dormitory, many of the residents claimed to hear loud noises in the vacant rooms and could find no cause for the sounds. Sometimes they heard footsteps going up and down the stairs or the sound of music being played in the empty hall where Mary Sibley's piano was stored; they would often find furniture rearranged. It was also reported that lights would often turn on and off in parts of the building that were always closed up and locked

One summer when the school was empty, Sibley Hall was being renovated. There was no one in the building but workmen and all of the doors were kept locked. The men were busy one day on the lower floor when they heard the sounds of female voices upstairs, loud sounds like drawers being opened and closed, and noises like trunks being dragged across the floor. At quitting time, several of the men went upstairs to make sure the ladies could get out and to make sure they locked the doors as they left. They had assumed that several young ladies were upstairs doing some work of their own, but they found no one there. The upper floors were completely vacant.

There is another story that centers on the open staircase that rises up three floors through the building. Apparently, a young woman was hurrying down the steps one day and she tripped and then tumbled over the balcony. Rather than plunging to her death, or at least serious injury, she felt a pair of strong but gentle hands take hold of her and pull her back to safety. She turned to thank her rescuer and found that no one was there. The story soon began to circulate that it had been Mary Sibley who had saved her, still watching over her girls from the other side.

While many scoff at the ghostly tales of Mary Sibley (including officials of Lindenwood College), they have long been a part of the school's lore. And as at many other haunted schools, there have been some unexplained happenings at the college, which lead many to wonder whether the ghost stories may have some truth to them after all.

Years ago, campus legend stated that Mary Sibley always returned to the school every Halloween night. Some said that she would ride across the campus on her horse. Others claimed that she rose from the grave and walked through Sibley Hall. One year, a student decided to dress up in old-fashioned clothes like Mary Sibley and frighten the other girls. As she made her way into the hall where the piano was kept, she realized that she was not in the room alone. She looked up and saw a woman in a period dress. The woman turned around . . . and the student saw the face of Mary Sibley! The girl screamed and fainted dead away. Her Halloween prank had apparently been interrupted by the real thing!

Such a story might sound like the stuff of campus legend to many, but before you laugh too loudly, consider a similar story that was told by a man with no connection to the university at all. One year, around the holiday season, the man was at a program held at Sibley Chapel and went looking for a restroom for his young daughter. He was searching in vain until a woman in a "period costume" came downstairs and explained to him how to find the facilities. He never claimed to know who the woman was and, having no knowledge of the school, was not aware of the ghost stories told there. However, he later found out that there was no one present that evening in period clothing, and no one seemed to know what he was talking about when he mentioned the incident to staff members.

Could it have been the spirit of Mary Sibley, still watching over the college that she founded?

Legends of Zombie Road

The old roadway that has been dubbed "Zombie Road" (a name by which it was known at least as far back as the 1950s) was once listed on maps as Lawler Ford Road. Constructed in the late 1860s, the road, which was once merely gravel and dirt, was paved at some point years ago but it is now mostly impassable by automobile. It was originally built to provide access to the Meramec River and the railroad tracks alongside it.

In 1868, the Glencoe Marble Company was formed to work the limestone deposits in what is now the Rockwoods Reservation, located nearby. A sidetrack was laid from the deposits to the town of Glencoe and on to the Lawler Ford Road, crossing the property of James E. Yeatman. The sidetrack from the Pacific Railroad switched off the main line at Yeatman Junction and at this same location, the Lawler Ford Road ended at the river. There is no record as to where the name Lawler came from, but a ford did cross the river at this point. At times, a boat was used to ferry people across the river here, which is undoubtedly why the road was placed at this location.

The narrow road was used for some time by trucks that hauled quarry stone from railcars, but later it fell into disuse. Those who recall the road when it was more widely used have told me that the narrow, winding lane, which runs through roughly two miles of dense woods, was always enveloped in a strange silence and a half-light. Shadows were always long here, even on the brightest days, and it was always impossible to see past the trees and brush to what was coming around the next curve. I was told that if you were driving and met another car, one of you would have to back up to one of the few wide places, or even all the way to the beginning of the road, in order for the other one to pass.

Strangely, even those that I talked to who had no interest in ghosts or the unusual mentioned that Zombie Road was a spooky place. I was told that one of the strangest things about it was that it never looked the same or seemed the same length twice, even on the return trip from the dead-end point where the stone company's property started. "At times," one person told me, "we had the claustrophobic feeling that it would never end and that we would drive on forever into deeper darkness and silence."

Thanks to its secluded location, and the fact that it fell into disrepair and was abandoned, Lawler Ford Road gained a reputation in the 1950s as a local hangout for area teenagers to have parties and drink beer, and as a lovers' lane as well. Located in Wildwood, which was formerly Ellisville, and Glencoe, the road can be reached by taking Manchester Road out west of the city to Old State Road South. By turning left down Ridge Road toward the Ridge Meadows Elementary School, curiosity-seekers could find the road, which was just to the left of the school. For years, it was marked with a sign for Lawler Ford Road but the sign has since disappeared. Only a chained gate marks the entrance today.

The road saw quite a lot of traffic in the early years of its popularity and occasionally still sees a traveler or two today. Most that come here now are not looking for a party. Instead, they come looking for the unexplained. Lawler Ford Road has gained a reputation for being haunted. Numerous legends and stories sprang up about the place, from the typical tales of murdered boyfriends and killers with hooks for hands to more specific tales of a local killer who was dubbed the "Zombie." He was said to live in an old dilapidated shack by the river and would attack young lovers who came there looking for someplace quiet and out of the way. As time passed, the stories of this madman were told and retold and eventually the name of Lawler Ford Road was largely forgotten and it was replaced with "Zombie Road," the name by which it is still known today.

There are many other stories as well, from ghostly apparitions in the woods to visitors who have vanished without a trace. There are also stories about a man who was killed here by a train in the 1970s and who now haunts the road and that of a mysterious old woman who yells at passersby from a house at the end of the road. There is another legend about a boy who fell from the bluffs along the river and died but whose body was never found. His ghost is also believed to haunt the area. And there are enough tales of Native American spirits and modern-day devil worshippers here to fill another book entirely.

But is there any truth to these tales, or any historical event that might explain how the ghost stories got started? Believe it or not, there may just be a kernel of truth to the legends of Zombie Road—and real-life paranormal experiences taking place as well.

The region around Zombie Road was once known as Glencoe. Today, it is a small village on the banks of the Meramec River and most of its residents live in houses that were once summer cottages. Most of the other houses are from the era when Glencoe was a bustling railroad and quarrying community. However, the days of prosperity have long since passed it by, and years ago, the village was absorbed by the larger town of Wildwood.

There is no record of the first inhabitants in the region, but they were likely the Native Americans who built the mounds that existed for centuries at the site of present-day St. Louis. The mound city that once existed there was one of the largest in North America and at its peak boasted more than forty thousand occupants. It is believed that the Native Americans relied heavily on the Meramec River and its surrounding forests for food. It is also believed that the area around Glencoe, because of the game and fresh water, was a stopping point for the Indians as they made their way to the flint quarries in present-day Jefferson County.

After the Mound Builders vanished from the area, the Osage, Missouri, and Shawnee Indians came to the region and mined the quarries for flint for making scrapers, weapon points, and other stone tools. They also hunted and fished along the Meramec River. The Shawnee had been invited into what was then the Louisiana region by the Spanish governor. Many of them settled west of St. Louis and they were, for a time, major suppliers of game to the settlement.

Many other tribes passed through the region as they were moved out of their original lands in the east, but no records exist of any of them ever staying near Glencoe. This is because the area was a pivotal point for travelers, Indians and settlers alike. The history of the region may explain why sightings and encounters of Native American ghosts have taken place along Lawler Ford Road. As we know that a ford once existed here (a shallow point in the river that was more easily navigated), it's likely that the road leading down to the river was once an Indian trail. The early settlers had a tendency to turn the already-existing trails into roads, which may have been what happened with the Lawler Ford Road. If the Native Americans left an impression behind here, in their travels, hunts, or quests for flint, that could be the reason Indian spirits are still encountered here today.

The first white settler in the area was Ninian Hamilton from Kentucky. He arrived near Glencoe around 1800 and obtained a settler's land grant. He built a house and trading post and became one of the wealthiest and most influential men of the period. In those days, the Meramec River bottoms were heavily forested and made up of steep hills and sharp bluffs. The river flooded frequently and the fords that existed were only usable during times of low water. There were no bridges or ferries that crossed the river, except for one far to the southeast. The trappers and traders that traveled west of St. Louis, like the Indians before them, came on horseback along the ridge route that later became Manchester Road. It skirted the Meramec and was high enough that it was not subject to flooding. Because of this, it passed directly by Hamilton's homestead and the trading post that he established there. With the well-used trail just outside his back door, as well as nearby fish, game, and fresh springwater, Hamilton's post prospered.

Hamilton later built some gristmills, an important resource for settlers in those days, near his trading post. One of the mills that Hamilton started was later replaced by a water mill for tanning leather by Henry McCullough, who had a tannery and shoemaking business that not only supplied the surrounding area but also allowed him to ship large quantities of leather to his brother in the south. McCullough was also a Kentuckian and purchased his land from Hamilton. He later served as the justice of the peace for about thirty years and as a judge for the county court from 1849 to 1852. He was married three times before he died in 1853; one of his wives was a sister of Ninian Hamilton. This wife, Della Hamilton McCullough, was killed in 1876 after being struck by a railroad car on the spur line from the Rockwoods Reservation.

It has been suggested that perhaps the death of Della Hamilton McCullough was responsible for the legend that has grown up around Zombie Road about the ghost of the person who was run over by a train. The story of this phantom has been circulating for at least three decades now but there is no record of anyone being killed on the train tracks in modern times. In fact, the only railroad death around Glencoe is that of Henry McCullough's unfortunate wife. Could it be her ghost that has been linked to Zombie Road?

The railroads are another vital connection between Glencoe and the stories of Lawler Ford Road. The first lines reached the area in 1853 when a group of passengers on flatcars arrived behind a steam locomotive called the St. Louis. A rail line had been constructed along the Meramec River, using two tunnels, and connected St. Louis to Franklin, which was later re-named Pacific, Missouri. The tiny station house at Franklin was little more than a shack in the wilderness at that time, but bands played and people cheered as the train pulled into the station.

Around this same time, tracks had been extended along the river, passing through what would be Glencoe. The site was likely given its name by Scottish railroad engineer James P. Kirkwood, who laid out the route. The name has its origins in Old English; "glen" means "a narrow valley" and "coe" means "grass."

Only a few remnants of the original railroad can be found today. The old tracks can still be seen at the end of Zombie Road and it is along these tracks that the railroad ghost is believed to walk. There have been numerous accounts over the years of a translucent figure in white that walks up the abandoned line and then disappears. Those who claim to have seen it say that the phantom glows with bluish-white light and disappears as soon anyone tries to approach it. The identity of this ghost remains a mystery, but despite the stories of a possible death in the 1970s, the presence is most likely the lingering spirit of Della McCullough.

One of the first passengers to make the trip west on the rail line from St. Louis was James E. Yeatman. He was one of the leading citizens of St. Louis and was the founder of the Mercantile Library, president of Merchants Bank, and an early proponent of extending the railroads west of the Mississippi. He was active in both business and charitable affairs in St. Louis and was a major force behind the Western Sanitary Commission during the Civil War. This large volunteer group provided hospital boats and medical services and looked to other needs of the wounded on both sides of the conflict. The world's first hospital railroad car is attributed to this group.

After the death of Ninian Hamilton in 1856, his heirs sold his land to A. S. Mitchell, who in turn sold it to James Yeatman. Yeatman built a large frame home on the property and dubbed it "Glencoe Park." The mansion burned to the ground in 1920 while under the ownership of Alfred Carr and Angelica Yeatman Carr, the daughter of James Yeatman. The Carrs moved into the stone guesthouse on the property, which also burned in 1954. It was later rebuilt and restored and still remains in the Carr family.

The village of Glencoe was laid out in 1854 by Woods, Christy & Co. and in 1883, it contained "a few houses and a small store, but for about a year has had no post office." At the time the town was created, Woods, Christy & Co. also erected a gristmill and sawmill at Glencoe that operated until about 1868. Woods, Christy & Co. had been a large dry goods company in St. Louis. There is a tradition in the Christy family that the early settlers traded land for goods and materials. This firm ceased operation as a dry goods company about 1856.

One of the many prominent St. Louis citizens who traveled through Glencoe during the middle and late 1800s was Winston Churchill, (not the British statesman but the American author) who went on to write a number of best-selling romantic novels in the early 1900s. One of the most popular, *The Crisis*, was set partially at Glencoe. The novel, which Churchill acknowledged was based on the activities of James E. Yeatman, depicts the struggles and conflicts in St. Louis during the critical years of the Civil War. It is believed that Angelica Yeatman Carr was his model for the heroine, Miss Virginia Carvel. The first edition of the book was published in 1901 and was followed by subsequent editions.

Copies can still be found on dusty shelves in used and antiquarian bookstores today.

In 1868, the Glencoe Marble Company was formed and the previously mentioned sidetrack was added to the railroad, running alongside the river. The tracks ran past where Lawler Ford Road ended and it's likely that wagons were used to haul quarry stone up the road.

During the Civil War, the city of St. Louis found itself in the predicament of being loyal to the Union in a state that was predominately dedicated to the Confederate cause. For this reason, men who were part of what was called the Home Guard were stationed along the roads and trails leading into the city with instructions to turn back Southern sympathizers by any means necessary. As a result, Confederate spies, saboteurs, and agents often had to find less-trafficked paths to get in and out of the St. Louis area. One of the lesser-known trails led to and away from the ford across the Meramec River near Glencoe. This trail would later become known as Lawler Ford Road.

As information about the trail's existence reached the leaders of the militia forces, troops from the Home Guard began to be stationed at the ford. The trail here led across the river and to the small town of Crescent, which was later dubbed "Rebel Bend" because of the number of Confederates who passed through it and found sanctuary there.

After the militia forces set up their lines, the river became very dangerous to cross. However, since there were so few fords across the Meramec, many attempted to cross there anyway, often with dire results. According to the stories, a number of men died there in skirmishes with the Home Guard. Could this violence explain some of the hauntings that are now said to occur along Zombie Road?

Many of the people whom I have talked with about the strange happenings here speak of unsettling feelings and the sensation of being watched. They also tell of eerie sounds, inexplicable noises, and even disembodied footsteps. Many have spoken of being "followed" as they walk along the trail, as though someone is keeping pace with them just on the edge of the woods. Strangely, no one is ever seen. In addition, it is not uncommon for visitors to also report seeing shapes and shadows of presences in the woods.

On many occasions, these shapes have been mistaken for actual people until the hiker goes to confront them and finds that there is no one there. It's possible that the violence, bloodshed, and trauma of the Civil War left its mark on this site, as many believe the shapes in the woods may be the sentries and soldiers who died in the local fighting.

Visitors to Lawler Ford Road today will often end their journey at the Meramec River, which has also played a part in the legends and tales of Zombie Road. It was at Yeatman Junction that one of the first large-scale gravel operations on the Meramec River began. Gravel was taken from the banks of the Meramec and moved on railcars into St. Louis. The first record of this operation is in the middle 1850s. Later, steam dredges were used, to be supplanted by diesel or gasoline dredges later still, to extract gravel from the channel and from artificial lakes dug into the south bank. This continued, apparently without interruption, until the 1970s.

The quarries were used until the demise of the gravel operation in the 1970s. The last railroad tracks were removed from around Glencoe when the spur line to the gravel pit was taken out. Some have cited the railroads as the source for some of the hauntings along Zombie Road. In addition to the wandering spirit that is believed to be Della McCullough, it is possible that some of the other restless ghosts may be those of victims of accidents along the rail lines. Sharp bends in the tracks at Glencoe were the sites of frequent derailments that were later recalled by local residents. The Carr family had a number of photographs in their collection of these deadly accidents. It finally got so bad that service was discontinued on the tracks that led around the bend in the river. It has been speculated that perhaps the victims of train accidents may still be lingering here and might explain how the area got such a reputation for tragedy and hauntings.

Many visitors also claim to have had strange experiences near the old shacks and deteriorating homes located along the beach area at the end of the trail. One of the long-standing legends of the place mentions the ghost of an old woman who screams at people from the doorways of one of the old houses. However, upon investigation, the old woman is never there.

The houses here date back to about 1900, when the area around Glencoe served as a resort community. The Meramec

River's "clubhouse era" lasted until about 1945. Many of the cottages were then converted to year-round residences, but others were simply left to decay in the woods. This is the origin of the old houses that are located off Zombie Road but it does not explain the ghostly old woman and the other apparitions that have been encountered here. Could they be former residents? Perhaps this haunting on the old roadway has nothing to do with the violence and death of the past but rather with happy memories from the time the area was a resort community. Perhaps some of these former residents returned to their cottages after death because the resort homes were places where they knew peace and contentment in life.

When I first began researching the history of Lawler Ford Road, I have to confess that I started with the idea that the "Zombie Road" was little more than an urban legend, created from the vivid imaginations of several generations of teenagers. I never expected to discover the violent history of the area, or anything that might substantiate the tales of ghosts and supernatural occurrences along this wooded road. It was easy to find people who believed in the legends of Zombie Road, but I never expected to be one of those who came to be convinced.

As time has passed, I have learned that there is more to this spooky place than first meets the eye and that it goes beyond mere legends linked to the old lovers' lane. For those who doubt that ghosts can be found along Zombie Road, I encourage you to spend just one evening there, along the dark paths and under the looming trees. You just might find that your mind has been changed.

As the famous quote from *The Haunting* states: "The supernatural is something that isn't supposed to happen, but it does happen." And I believe that it happens along Zombie Road.

Meramec Caverns

I grew up with a fascination for caves. I have lost count of the number of sidetrips that I have taken over the years after spotting a lurid sign on the road advertising some great "wonder under the earth." The first cave that I remember visiting as a child was Meramec Caverns. Growing up, I often saw signs and roadside markers (usually painted on the roof of a decrepit old barn) that advertised the cave as "Jesse James' Hideout," which made it even more appealing to a young boy. As an adult, I know that the outlaw's connection to the cave is a bit tenuous, but it's still an appealing place.

And it became even more appealing when I heard the stories about the ghosts.

The cave that became known many years later as Meramec Caverns was first discovered by Europeans in 1720. A French settler named Phillip Renault, who was based in Kaskaskia in the country of the Illinois Indians, was told of a hole in the earth along the Meramec River by an Osage Indian guide. The hole opened into a large room that had been providing Native Americans with shelter from the weather for generations. The Indians told of walls that sparkled with yellow metal. Believing that the "yellow metal" might be gold, Renault went in search of the cave. There was no gold there, he discovered, but there was saltpeter, a substance that could also make a man very rich in those days.

Saltpeter, also known as niter, is potassium (or sodium) nitrate. When it is combined and ground together with charcoal and sulfur, correctly and in the right quantities, it produces black gunpowder. Missouri has nineteen caves where saltpeter was once found, and the one Renault was told of turned out to be one of the largest. It was dubbed Saltpeter Cave and Renault's mining company operated there between 1720 and 1740, generating large quantities of a product necessary for hunting, defense, and war. Later, disputes over the cave's saltpeter operations led to violence, especially during the Civil War, when it was allegedly claimed by both Confederate and Union troops.

The Civil War plunged rural Missouri and the Ozarks into chaos. Into this bloody time came the James Gang, the Youngers, and a slew of lesser outlaws. During and after the war, they robbed banks and railroads and wreaked such havoc that Missouri became known for a time as the "Outlaw State." While many scoff at the legends that connect Jesse James to Missouri caves, others claim such stories are true. Victims of the many crime sprees of the day were never sure which outlaws were riding with who and wild imaginations and false stories often led to

Jesse James being connected to just about every robbery that took place. Some of the stories even had him committing robberies in two different states at the same time. When members of outlaw gangs were spotted in the cave regions of the state, people often assumed that local caves were being used as hideouts—and so the stories grew.

With James being the best-known outlaw in Missouri's history, it's no surprise that his presence was often claimed when the show cave industry sprang up in the region in the 1880s and 1890s. James had been killed in 1882, so he was still fresh in the minds of the cave operators and of the people who came to see the caves. Many show cave developers began to promote their own outlaw legends to add mystery and suspense to the histories of their attractions. But no other cave has embraced the story of Jesse James in the way that Meramec Caverns has.

By the 1890s, the people of nearby Stanton began using Saltpeter Cave as a place to escape the summer heat. In 1895, a man named D.N. Gideon and his partner, Joseph Schmuke, began holding parties and dances in the "Ballroom" section of the cave. The events reached a wide audience. Gideon and Schmuke connected with A. Hilton, the passenger traffic manager of the Frisco Railroad, and who eagerly promoted the events as a way to fill seats on the trains that ran between St. Louis and Springfield.

Gideon was a grocer who owned a general store in Stanton, and Schmuke owned a hotel and operated a saloon in town, which allowed them to handily profit from the parties. They advertised Saltpeter Cave as a "grand work of nature."

The crowds that attended the events entered the cave through the spacious main entrance and walked about three hundred feet to enter an immense, circular chamber with a hard-packed, smooth floor. There were two large wings to the Ballroom and the temperature was a pleasant 60 degrees all year round. Gideon and Schmuke had constructed a dance floor, secured lanterns along the walls, and built a bar and a platform for the musicians. They cleaned up the old wagon road to the cave so that it was easy to get to.

The parties became very successful and word spread up and down the Frisco Railroad line. People came from St. Louis and Springfield to attend and hardly a summer weekend passed without some sort of event at the cave. Gideon and Schmuke made so much money that they continued to offer summer dances at Saltpeter Cave until 1910.

Things changed dramatically at the cave in 1901, however. During a caving expedition, explorers at Saltpeter Cave made a major discovery, uncovering unbelievably beautiful upper levels of the cave. Up until that time, the cave had been thought to end just beyond the Ballroom. But the new portion of the cave soon became a major attraction. People who attended the parties were now able to tour the upper sections of the cave, which became a forerunner to the show cave status that the site would achieve starting in 1933.

Meramec Caverns became a show cave under the operation of a man named Lester Benton Dill. He grew up on a farm along the Meramec River and, as a boy, spent many summers exploring the caves of the river valley. Visitors who came to the area were quick to offer pocket money to Dill and his brothers to act as local guides.

After the dedication of Meramec State Park in 1928, Dill's father, Thomas Benton Dill, became the first park superintendent. The family was able to convince the state to open Fisher Cave as a special attraction in the park and Lester Dill operated the cave as a concessionaire. But in the early 1930s, a change in state politics cost Thomas Dill his position as superintendent and Lester lost the cave operation. He immediately started looking for a nearby wild cave—outside the park property—that he could commercialize. He found the perfect location in Saltpeter Cave.

On May 1, 1933, Dill opened Saltpeter Cave to the public as Meramec Caverns. With help from his family, he was able to transform it into one of the greatest show caves in Missouri history and cemented it as one of the best-known caves in the country. He continued to explore the cave, opening up additional sections over the years, and wildly promoted the cave through the use of billboards, painted barns, and bumper stickers (becoming the first person ever to use bumper stickers to publicize an attraction). Dill also bought other local caves, including Onondaga Cave, and became known as "America's Number One Caveman." Dill passed away in 1980, leaving behind a rich legacy in the Meramec River Valley.

The stories of strange happenings at Meramec Caverns began to be told in the late 1940s. The guides don't offer these stories voluntarily but will usually relate odd events when asked. Many of the tales seem to connect to events of the past, perhaps repeating themselves over and over again. Many staff members and visitors speak of hearing voices and footsteps in the cave when no one is there. Such events could be dismissed as echoes encountered by people who are not familiar with the acoustics of caves, but what about the reports from experienced cavers? Others tell of the sounds of music and laughter—perhaps lingering remnants of the parties held in the cave in the late 1800s.

One cave guide related the fact that the last tour of the day often hears mysterious voices coming from the dark corridors of the cave. In busy attractions like Meramec Caverns, it's not uncommon to hear the sounds of the cave tour in front of you or behind you, but what about when it's the last tour of the day? Why do visitors hear voices from a tour that simply isn't there?

A few people who have visited Meramec Caverns have reported seeing an apparition of a smiling man. He is there one moment and gone the next. Lights flicker in the cave when this ghost puts in an appearance, even when there is no one near the switch. Some have suggested that this ghost is the spirit of Lester Dill, who never truly left the cave that he loved so much. Does he watch over his beloved cavern, even after death?

Diamonds Restaurant

Journeying along old Route 66 today is like taking a trip back in time, but it's a time capsule where much of the past lies tragically in ruin. One Missouri location along the stretch of highway known as the "Mother Road" was a place built from dreams and lovingly embraced by the travelers along Route 66. It's now a silent stone building at the fork of Old Highway 100 and Highway AT in Villa Ridge. It was once a vibrant and thriving place, but today, only the ghosts remain.

There is no greater highway in the history of America than Route 66. For millions of people, it represents a treasure trove of memories and a link to the days of two-lane highways, family vacations, lunches at roadside tables, and little diners. It conjures up images of souvenir shops, tourist traps, cozy motor courts, and cheesy roadside attractions that have since crumbled into oblivion. Route 66 makes us think of rusty steel bridges, flickering neon signs, drive-in theaters, and more. It's America's favorite highway, even though officially it no longer exists.

Route 66 began simply with the needs of a growing nation and the vision of one man. In 1924, Oklahoma Highway Commissioner Cyrus Avery, who was nationally known among transportation officials, was recruited by the U.S. Bureau of Public Roads to help develop a new system of interstate highways. Avery accepted the bureau's offer and throughout 1925 worked with a committee to connect hundreds of existing roads into a nationwide network. It was the dawn of the American automobile. Cars had finally become available to the average person and families were taking to the road like never before. They wanted to travel and Cyrus Avery was one of the people who helped them do it.

Avery was given broad authority and made sure that one of the chosen routes, designed with the backing of officials in Illinois and Missouri, cut directly across his home state of Oklahoma as part of a Chicago-to-Los Angeles thoroughfare. When first presented, this unconventional route was not well received. It took months for Avery to overcome the committee's reluctance and even when they finally accepted it, there was more disagreement, this time over the proposed numbering assignment (Avery initially wanted the highway to be called Route 60). After much debate, Route 66 was designated on November 11, 1926.

To help promote the new highway, Avery organized the U.S. 66 Highway Association shortly after leaving office. Through its efforts, Route 66 was soon entrenched as America's premier highway. Hard times came about just as the highway was beginning, and during the decade of the Dust Bowl and the Great Depression, it became a route of escape for thousands of families who moved westward from Oklahoma, Texas, and Arkansas. The plight of these migrants and travelers, seeking salvation from the drought, was immortalized in John Steinbeck's *The Grapes of Wrath.* In the book, he called Route 66 "the mother road, the road of flight." The nickname stuck and for many years, Route 66 was seen as a passage to hope for struggling "Okies" and those who were down on their luck.

During World War II, Route 66 became a military conduit, providing a fast-moving passage for men, munitions, and equipment to move about the country. The continuous convoys kept the highway busy and the pockets of merchants filled. In spite of this, however, Route 66, a road designed for civilian travel, paid the price in the wear and tear caused by the military vehicles. It eventually weakened and began to decline, a development that did not go unnoticed in Washington. Officials were already considering a wider and faster highway system that could handle the toughest traffic demands. By the time the war ended, the demise of Route 66, although still years away, had become inevitable.

For a few years, though, a return to peacetime brought new prosperity and a tourism boom to America. Spurred on by Bobby Troup's musical hit "Get Your Kicks on Route 66," people were anxious to travel and the highway profited. As traffic on the road increased, new businesses sprang up and an explosion of tourist traps, curio shops, and neon signs began to appear in just about every town on Route 66's path. Motor courts became "motels," diners became "restaurants," and general stores changed into "trading posts." Hundreds of new billboards helped to spread the word about these booming businesses.

It was an era of good times that is now looked back on with nostalgia, but it was never meant to last. By the middle 1950s, the interstates were making their way west and over the next fifteen years, Route 66 began to vanish. It was ripped up, downgraded, and realigned—and the hundreds of towns that were dependent on the highway's traffic were slowly strangled in the process. Many of them became ghost towns, fading reminders of the days that once were. By the end of the 1960s, with the damage done, "America's Main Street" had ceased to be a through route to California. It was not officially decommissioned, though, until the stubborn citizens of Williams, Arizona, the last town to be bypassed, lost a legal battle to stop it in 1984.

Although long stretches of Route 66 still remain today, most of it is a hard-to-define mix of original roadbed, access roads, abandoned fragments, and lost highways. It has been reconfigured in so many ways that even diehard travelers can sometimes become lost and turned around as they try and follow the road's often lonely miles. But the memories remain and so do some of the old sites. Along the old roads are abandoned stores, broken and dead neon signs for businesses that have long since vanished, and even creaky motor courts that are sometimes still eking out a living from travelers that are now few and far between.

And in many of those now-quiet places, the ghosts of the past remain too.

One such place is the old Diamonds Restaurant, which was once a Missouri fixture on the Mother Road. The restaurant actually started as fruit and vegetable stand in 1927. An enterprising young man named Spencer Groff started the stand to get a share of the money being spent by Route 66 travelers; it eventually did so well that it blossomed into a restaurant and mercantile store called The Diamonds. The place was designed in the shape of a baseball diamond. Groff sold gas from Phillips 66 pumps and rented out twenty-five cabins across the road to tourists. The eatery, which gained fame as "The World's Largest Roadside Restaurant," featured scores of tables and three U-shaped lunch counters with attendants. The menu ranged from burgers to turkey dinners.

In 1947, the restaurant burned down. Groff gave up on the place and turned the business over to one of his longtime employees. The Diamonds was rebuilt and thanks to Route 66, prospered into the 1960s. Unfortunately, though, the completion of the interstate brought about the end of the old highway. After the new road was opened in 1968, a new Diamonds was built near the interstate. The old icon, which had been rebuilt after the fire, was sold and became the Tri-County Restaurant and Truck Stop.

If there were already ghosts at The Diamonds, they refused to leave with the rest of the traffic and stayed behind at what was once an icon of Route 66. Today, all that remains of the "new" Diamonds is the 1968 sign. The original building has long since been torn down, though what became the Tri-County Truck Stop remains. Truckers became the mainstay for the old Diamonds until newer and more accessible truck stops opened along the interstate. Then the all-hours restaurant became a hangout for the late-night bar crowd and for even seedier folks. During its time as primarily a stop for truck drivers, the second floor of the building was renovated into rooms and showers and became a hangout for hitchhikers and prostitutes.

Stories of ghosts began to emerge from the Tri-County Truck Stop in the early 1970s. Employees and customers began telling of being touched by unseen hands, hearing voices, and seeing shadowy figures that shouldn't have been there. Over the course of the next two decades, eerie accounts were told of the basement and of the apparitions seen moving around in the darkness there. Objects moved about on their own, lights and appliances turned on and off, and later, staff members told of frequent sightings of a man wearing a plaid shirt and tan pants who would appear and disappear at random. Others claimed to see the spirits of a man and a woman covered in blood, which some interpret as a spectral reenactment of a murder that was never reported. Things got so bad at the truck stop in the 1990s that local residents began claiming that the ghosts of the building were actually spilling out of the place and into the surrounding area. They told of ghosts in their homes and of a hitchhiker on Highway 100 that would mysteriously vanish after being picked up. He always asked to be dropped off at the Tri-County Truck Stop and then inexplicably vanished from the car.

Eventually, the Tri-County Restaurant and Truck Stop became a victim of the times and closed its doors. It's now a ghost in its own right, a vacant and abandoned shell of what it once was. The windows are boarded over and the glory of yesterday is now long past. Once has to wonder what will happen to the place now that time has passed it by. And what will become of the ghosts?

Along the Mississippi

Ghosts of Ste. Genevieve

Founded around 1735 by French settlers from the Illinois country, Ste. Genevieve is the oldest permanent European settlement in Missouri. It is a place of old, rich history, connected to the often violent and deadly Mississippi River; thanks to the scores of people who have called this place home, it is also known for its ghosts.

The first inhabitants of the region—including a group of the Native Americans known as the Mississippi culture—had been living there for more than a thousand years. When the first settlers arrived, though, no Indian tribe lived along the river banks. Driven west of the Mississippi by hostile Indians and the exhausted soil of their older Illinois villages, the French arrived on the site of the future Ste. Genevieve and named the small village for the patron saint of Paris.

At the time of its founding, Ste. Genevieve was the last of three French settlements in the mid-Mississippi Valley region. About five miles northeast of Ste. Genevieve was Fort de Chartres, in Illinois country; Kaskaskia, which became Illinois' first capital upon statehood, was located about five miles to the southeast.

Prairie du Rocher and Cahokia were two other early local French colonial settlements on the east side of the river.

In 1762, with the signing of the Treaty of Fontainebleau, France secretly ceded the west bank of the river to Spain, and it became part of Louisiana. The Spanish moved the capital of Upper Louisiana from Fort de Chartres fifty miles upriver to St. Louis, Missouri. Although under Spanish control for more than forty years, Ste. Genevieve retained its French language, customs, and character.

In 1763, the French ceded the land east of the Mississippi to Great Britain in the Treaty of Paris, which ended Europe's Seven Years' War (known in the United States as the French and Indian War). French-speaking people from Canada and from east of the Mississippi flocked to Ste. Genevieve, turning the place into a thriving community.

The first major bloodshed in Ste. Genevieve came in the 1770s when the Little Osage and Missouri tribes began raiding the town and stealing horses. But the fur trade, marriages between French men and Native American women, and other commercial dealings created many ties between Native Americans and the French. During the 1780s, Shawnee and Delaware migrated to the west side of the Mississippi following the American victory in the Revolutionary War. The tribes established villages south of Ste. Genevieve. The Peoria also moved near Ste. Genevieve in the 1780s but had a peaceful relationship with the village.

It was not until the 1790s that the violence returned to the town when the Big Osage tribe began attacking the settlement, as well as its Shawnee and Peoria allies. Repeated raids occurred and a number of settlers were killed. Spanish leaders made plans to launch a counterattack against the Big Osage, but lacked the men and arms to carry it out. In 1794, Carondelet, the Spanish governor at New Orleans, appointed the Chouteau brothers of St. Louis to begin exclusive trade with the Big Osage. They built a fort and trading post to deal with the Indians in their own territory; while it did not stop the raids on Ste. Genevieve completely, the Chouteau brothers did manage to end most of the violence.

After the great flood of 1795, the town moved from its early location on the river's floodplain to its present location two miles north and a half mile inland. It continued to prosper as a village devoted to agriculture, especially wheat, maize, and tobacco production. Most of the families were farmers, although some were fairly wealthy. The village raised sufficient grain to send many tons of flour annually for sale to Lower Louisiana and New Orleans, which helped the colonists in that region survive, as they could not grow grains there. In 1807, the secretary of the Louisiana Territory, Frederick Bates, noted Ste. Genevieve was "the most wealthy village in Louisiana."

The town of Ste. Genevieve is a place where history survives into the present. It exists in its homes and architecture and, according to many, its ghosts.

The oldest buildings of Ste. Genevieve, built in a style called "French Creole colonial," date back to Spanish rule. The most distinctive buildings of this period were the "vertical wooden post" constructions where walls of buildings were built based on wood "posts" either dug into the ground (*poteaux en terre,* "posts in the ground") or set on a raised stone or brick foundation (*poteaux sur solle,* "posts on a sill"). Of the vertical slab houses, the most distinctive are *poteaux en terre* buildings where the walls made of upright wooden slabs do not support the floor. The floor is supported by separate stone pillars. Partially set into dirt, the walls of such buildings were extremely vulnerable to flood damage, termites, and rot. Most of the oldest buildings in town are *poteaux sur solle.* The town's oldest structure is the Louis Bolduc House, which was built in 1770 at Ste. Genevieve's original riverfront location. Portions of the house were relocated in 1785 and the house was expanded at the new town site. The new house was completed in 1793 and had three large rooms, a sign of Bolduc's wealth.

One of the most famous haunted houses in town is the La Maison de Guibord House, which was built in 1806. The house was originally constructed along the river in 1784 by Jacques Dubreuil Guibord, a French merchant. The house became a landmark on the river and a meeting place for military officers during the Spanish regime.

The first encounter with ghosts in the house was reported by Jules Valle in 1893, when he claimed that he saw three phantoms in Spanish clothing. The men were only seen from the waist up and they quickly disappeared. Since then, they have been seen many times, but they apparently do not haunt the house alone. In more recent times, the house has become a historic site and staff members say that strange things still occur in the house, like moving objects and unexplained crashing sounds. Footsteps have also been heard pacing back and forth in empty rooms and cries have been heard in the rear rooms, which were once used as slave quarters.

Another ghostly spot in Ste. Genevieve is Memorial Cemetery, the oldest burial ground in the city. It is located at the end of Merchant Street and while not large, contains nearly five thousand souls—many of which reportedly do not rest in peace. The cemetery was started in 1787 and it became the burial place for many of the city's most prominent leaders and settlers.

By the late 1870s, it had become seriously overcrowded and many complained that new graves were disturbing the graves of those who had been buried previously. The cemetery was declared a public nuisance and a health hazard in 1879 and was finally closed in 1881.

There was one last burial after that date, however. Odile Pratte Valle, wife of city leader Felix Valle, was determined to spend eternity next to her husband. He had died in 1877 and had been interred in Memorial Cemetery. Madame Valle approached the city fathers with an attractive proposal shortly after the cemetery was closed. She would donate a large tract of land for use as a cemetery if she could be buried next to her husband in the closed cemetery when she passed away. The proposal was accepted and she died at the age of ninety, fifteen years after the cemetery had been closed down.

Many of the occupants of the graves here are unknown and the cemetery has been largely abandoned and neglected since 1882. None of the old wooden markers remain and most of the iron French crosses have been stolen. The majority of the smaller monuments have also disappeared, lost to the ravages of time and the elements. In recent years, a foundation has formed to try to protect the cemetery from further damage.

The years of ruin and abandonment have given birth to a number of legends about the cemetery. The most popular sprang up in the early 1900s when rumors stated that the spirits of the people buried in Memorial Cemetery played a deadly game of hide-and-seek every Halloween night. It was said that anyone who ventured into the cemetery and saw this event would go to their own grave before the next Halloween!

Rockcliffe Mansion & Other Hannibal Haunts

In 1903, Mark Twain wrote a story about a strange presence that he encountered one night in an abandoned mansion. In the tale, entitled "A Ghost Story," he wrote, "I seemed groping among the tombs and invading the privacy of the dead, that first night I climbed up to my quarters. For the first time in my life, a superstitious dread came over me . . . I became conscious that my chamber was invaded—that I was not alone."

It's no surprise that Mark Twain had a macabre bent to some of his tales, since he grew up in the Mississippi River village of Hannibal, where ghost stories are almost as common as the boats that float past town.

Stories of ghosts have been around Hannibal for many years and spirits are believed to walk the streets, wander the local graveyards, and lurk ominously in the darkest corners of the small town. But there are several locations in town that have gained infamy over the years for otherworldly presences.

One of them is the Garden House Bed and Breakfast, which is located along the mansion-lined Millionaire's Row on South Fifth Street. The inn is the former residence of Albert J. Pettibone, the wealthy son of a local sawmill founder, who died at the age of twenty-nine. According to the current owners, as well as many overnight guests, Pettibone still wanders the halls and upstairs rooms at night.

Another location is the LaBinnah Bistro, which is connected to the still-unsolved Stillwell murder, a bloody homicide that occurred back in 1888. One dark night, Amos J. Stillwell, one of the city's wealthiest residents, left a card game at the home of Hannibal's mayor, which is the building where the restaurant is now located. One of the men he played cards with that night was Dr. Joseph Hearne—a man rumored to be having an affair with Stillwell's wife, Fanny, who was nearly two decades younger than her husband. After the card game, Stillwell and his wife tucked in their two small children and went to bed.

According to her testimony, Fanny awoke in the middle of the night to see a shadowy figure standing over the bed with an ax. The person spoke aloud, "Is that you, Fanny?" before swinging the ax and crushing Stillwell's skull. The figure then disappeared out the window. Fanny fled from the house in her blood-soaked nightgown and ran down the street, knocking on doors and calling for help. She asked the neighbors to call Dr. Hearne; when he arrived, he allegedly found her in a catatonic state. The police were summoned to the house, but when they walked in, they found that several well-meaning neighbors had already cleaned up much of the crime scene. The authorities searched far and wide for the killer but no real clues were ever found.

Meanwhile, one year after Stillwell was killed, Fanny and Dr. Hearne were married. The murder was never solved, but the people of Hannibal were convinced they knew what had happened. Dr. Hearne was arrested and placed on trial for the murder but the case was eventually dismissed for lack of evidence. His practice all but dried up, though, and Fanny was frequently harassed by people on the street. Eventually, public pressure forced them to move out of the area. In all likelihood, the Stillwell murder will remain unsolved forever.

Over the years, rumors of a haunting connected to the case have made the rounds. Owners and residents of what is now the LaBinnah Bistro maintain that the location is haunted, thanks to its link to the murder. The spirit of a mournful-looking man has often been seen in the house, crossing the room and walking into the kitchen before he disappears. He is, many believe, the ghost of Amos Stillwell, making the final fateful walk toward home— where his life ended in violence.

But Hannibal's most infamous haunted place looms high above the town, looking down from a rocky knoll at the river below. This imposing structure is Rockcliffe Mansion, a magnificent mansion that was built by Scottish immigrant and lumber baron John J. Cruikshank between 1898 and 1900. The house was built with supplies furnished by Cruikshank's own company, using all of the finest walnut, oak, and mahogany. The double-brick construction was the innovative design of Barnett, Haynes, and Barnett, a well-known firm from St. Louis. The interior of the home was designed with large rooms and impressive hallways and had Palladian windows and ten carved marble and tile fireplaces.

The house soon became known all over the state. The *St. Louis Post-Dispatch* called it "the finest home in Missouri" and author Mark Twain gave his "farewell to Hannibal" speech from the front steps of the mansion in 1902. Cruikshank and his wife and four daughters lived happily in the house until his death in 1924.

He died but, according to those who continue to see him, he has never left the mansion.

But his family did. Mrs. Cruikshank moved out of Rockcliffe after her husband's death in 1924 and she left about eighty percent of the family's furniture and belongings behind. The house was boarded up for the next forty-three years, slowly deteriorating with time. Two weeks before the mansion was finally going to be torn down, it was saved by three local families who have since restored it to its former glory. Today, Rockcliffe stands high on the knoll overlooking Hannibal and the Mississippi River and still contains many original artifacts, artwork, clothing, furniture, and personal items—and one enduring ghost.

After the mansion's renovations, the ghost of John Cruikshank has been encountered many times in the house. It's as if he simply refuses to let go of the place that he loved so much and literally built with his own two hands. He is often heard at night, coming in the creaking door of the servants' entrance, climbing the back staircase, and walking down the hallway to his bedroom. Startled occupants of the house never find a living person as the source of the sounds. He also manifests as the smell of cigar smoke—even though no one smokes in the mansion—and as an uncomfortable touch or the feeling as if someone has just brushed past.

But it's not just sounds and smells; Cruikshank has also made frequent appearances in his former home. Visitors and staff members of the bed-and-breakfast now located in the mansion sometimes walk into rooms and see him standing there. When they approach, he simply fades away. All of them describe the apparition as a short man with white hair and a goatee, wearing a brown suit and hat from the early 1900s. It is a perfect description of John Cruikshank!

Those who come face to face with him can always agree that while unnerving, there is nothing frightening about the ghost. He simply chose to stay behind at the one place in the world where he knew the greatest happiness—and he doesn't seem to have plans to go away anytime soon.

Mark Twain Cave

What young reader will ever forget the breathless events that occur at the climax of Mark Twain's classic story *The Adventures of Tom Sawyer*, as Injun Joe pursues Tom and Becky Thatcher through the dark confines of the cave? It was a part of the story that stuck with me long after I had placed the book back on the shelf. Later, I found out that the cave in the story was real. Twain had based it on a cave that was located just outside of his boyhood home of Hannibal. But nothing in the story about Tom Sawyer even comes close to chronicling the strange events that actually took place in this mysterious cave.

The cave that now bears the name of Mark Twain was discovered in 1819 by a local hunter and farmer named Jack Sims. He was out hunting and his dogs chased a panther into the cave. The cave turned out to be more than six miles long and, due to the cool temperatures inside, it came to be used as a town meeting hall and a venue for many parties and weddings during the humid summer months. It the 1950s, it even served as a bomb shelter for a time.

Today the cave is known as Mark Twain Cave in honor of the author who made it famous in the story of Tom Sawyer, but in the 1840s, it was named McDowell's Cave, for its owner: the infamous St. Louis doctor Joseph McDowell (see page 18).

The eccentric McDowell, the founder of the first medical college west of the Mississippi, had been raised in Kentucky before coming to Missouri. His formal education was at Transylvania College in Kentucky, where he studied under Dr. Samuel Brown, a professor of chemistry. Brown was an authority on saltpeter and the saltpeter caves in Kentucky, and he not only experimented

with the uses of saltpeter in medicine but encouraged his students to do so. He believed that the preservative qualities of the chemical had promising medical uses.

During the time when McDowell operated his medical school in St. Louis, it was nearly impossible to obtain cadavers to be dissected for medical research. He and his students raided the local graveyards for fresh corpses and this often ran him afoul of local residents. After what he believed was a supernatural encounter with the ghost of his mother, who saved him from a lynch mob that was after him for his latest theft, McDowell became fascinated with the spirit world. His newfound respect for the spirit world often affected the new ideas that he came up with.

In 1827, McDowell had married Amanda Virginia Drake of Mason County, Kentucky, who bore him ten children. After his encounter with the spirit, he began to be concerned about the eventual deaths of his family. He hated to think of their decay after death, so he planned to encase them in copper tubes and install them in niches inside of the medical college's main tower when they died. Later, however, when preserved bodies were discovered in Mammoth Cave in Kentucky, he became fascinated with the idea of placing the bodies in caves, where the natural powers of saltpeter might allow them to last indefinitely. He purchased the cave in Hannibal and it was here that he placed the body of his fourteen-year-old daughter who died of pneumonia. She was preserved inside of a cooper tube, lined with glass, which was filled with alcohol. She was hidden away inside of the cave, where McDowell assumed that she would be safe.

Unknown to McDowell, local children used the cave as a playground of sorts, often wandering about the maze of passages on warm afternoons. One of those local children was a young Samuel Clemens, who would go on to become known as Mark Twain. In his book *Life on the Mississippi*, he wrote about the cave and its curious occupant, "There is an interesting cave a mile or two below Hannibal. In my time, the person who then owned it turned it into a mausoleum for his daughter, age 14. The body was put into a copper cylinder filled with alcohol and this was suspended in one of the dismal avenues of the cave. The top of the cylinder was removable and it was a common thing for the baser order of tourists to drag the dead face into view and examine it and comment upon it."

The girl's body was left in the cave for two years, but the youths who broke into the cave to see her bragged about it to their friends, and weird rumors spread around Hannibal about what McDowell was doing in the cave. Alarmed, local men broke into the place and had a look for themselves. McDowell was eventually forced to remove the body. He then had her placed in a crypt on the Illinois side of the river next to his wife, who had recently died. He later wrote that he could see their resting place with a telescope from the cupola on top of the college.

The cave was eventually sold, and once Twain's stories of Tom Sawyer and Huckleberry Finn became popular, people began calling it Mark Twain Cave. The popularity of Twain's books generated public demand for access to the cave and it was commercialized in 1886. It is now the oldest show cave west of the Mississippi.

The remote section of the cave where McDowell's daughter was placed is not regularly shown to the touring public today but the tale of the body in the tube remains a spooky highlight of the tour. But is there more to this story than just the weird experiment?

Rumors persist that the cave is haunted by the ghost of McDowell's daughter. Tour guides have spoken of feeling an overwhelming cold chill, only to turn and see a young girl standing behind them. She is usually seen wearing a long white gown and standing in the hallway that leads back to what they call the McDowell Room. She smiles and then turns and walks away, and a moment later she is gone. Visitors to the cave, unaware of the unusual story, have also seen her on occasion. They are puzzled about the presence of a young woman in an old-fashioned dress, who vanishes into a section of the cave that is off-limits to tourists.

One has to wonder why the doctor's daughter might linger behind in a place that she never knew in life. Did her spirit stay with her body after it was moved to the cave? If so, then perhaps this means that Dr. McDowell's ideas about life after death were not so eccentric after all.

The Hunter-Dawson House

The Mississippi River town of Mew Madrid earned its place of infamy in American history during the winter of 1811–12, as the epicenter of one of the worst series of earthquakes ever recorded. Today, the reputation lingers—and so do the ghosts.

Strange things began to happen in the Missouri Territory in 1811. Residents along the Mississippi River near the settlement of New Madrid began reporting all manner of weird happenings. First, it was the animals. Livestock began to act nervous and excited. Dogs began to bark and howl and even the most domesticated of animals turned vicious. Wild animals began to act tame. Deer wandered out of the woods and up to the doors of cabins. Flocks of ducks and geese landed near people. It was unlike anything the local residents had ever seen before.

Soon, stories spread of eerie lights that were seen in the woods and in the hills. Strange, bluish-white flashes and balls of light were seen floating in the trees and cresting the nearby ridges.

The New Madrid earthquakes began at about two o'clock on the morning of December 16, 1811. The ground shook and heaved like waves on the ocean and the violent shock was accompanied by a loud sound like distant thunder. The violent trembling caused roofs to collapse, chimneys to fall, and items in homes to be thrown about, and numerous people were injured. Rocks and dirt collapsed along the bluffs of the Mississippi and in some places, sand and water were forced to the surface in frightening eruptions. In the darkness before dawn, no one had any idea just how much damage was being done.

Between the initial earthquake and sunrise, a number of lighter shocks occurred, followed by another violent shaking just as the sun was coming up. The terror that had taken over the local populace, as well as the animals in the region, was now, if possible, doubled. People began to flee in every direction, perhaps believing that there was less danger if they could get away from the river. Many were injured not from the shock of the earthquakes but in their haste in trying to escape.

Thousands of minor shocks and occasional stronger earthquakes were experienced during the following days and weeks. On January 23, 1812, at about 9:00 A.M., an earthquake comparable to the one in December took place. It was reportedly felt as far away as Boston. According to many accounts, the earth remained in continual agitation until February 4, when another strong quake occurred. Four quakes took place over the course of the next few days and then on February 7, around 4:00 A.M., another violent concussion shook the region. It was as if the gates of hell had opened in southeastern Missouri.

The February 7 earthquake caused two waterfalls to form on the Mississippi River near New Madrid and, for a short while, the Mississippi River ran backward until the mighty force of the water caused the falls to collapse. At first, the river had seemed to recede from its banks, and its waters gathered up in the center, leaving many boats stranded on bare sand. The water then rose fifteen to twenty feet and then expanded, rapidly rushing toward the shore and flowing over the banks. Boats that had been left on the sand were torn from their moorings and driven more than a quarter mile up a small creek. The river fell rapidly, as quickly as it had risen, and receded from the banks in such a torrent that it ripped away whole groves of cottonwood trees that had been growing along the shore. They were broken off with such precision that in some instances, people who had not witnessed the event refused to believe they had not been cut. Thousands of fish were stranded on the banks, left behind by the surging water.

During the hard shocks, the earth was torn to pieces. Hundreds of acres were covered over, in various depths, by the sand that came out of the fissures, great yawning gaps that opened up all over the countryside. Some of them closed immediately after vomiting up sand and water, but others remained as open wounds in fields, pastures, and forests.

After the February 7 earthquake, only weaker aftershocks took place, which still occur today.

No settlers were reported killed during the earthquakes, but many towns and cities experienced damage from the shaking ground. It is believed that the damage and death toll would have been much higher, perhaps at catastrophic levels, if the region had been more heavily populated at the time. In 1811, that portion of the Mississippi Valley was still sparsely inhabited frontier. If the area had been as populated as it is today, the New Madrid earthquakes would have been one of the worst disasters in American history. Terrifyingly, there is still a chance of this happening. Minor tremors still occur along what is known as the New Madrid Fault Line on an almost daily basis and scientists believe that another major quake is inevitable. When it might happen, though, is anyone's guess.

As time passed, the memory of those horror-filled days faded and New Madrid became a busy trading port on the river. Many merchants and businessmen moved to the area, including William Washington Hunter, a native of Virginia who settled in New Madrid with his wife, Amanda, in 1830. They became very successful in the mercantile business and opened a large dry goods store called the Crystal Palace. In addition, they opened a floating store that traveled to other nearby towns on the river. Hunter invested in land and eventually owned as much as fifteen thousand acres in four states.

The Hunters soon began planning a grand house. Using yellow cypress, cut at their own sawmill, hired workmen, along with the family's thirty-six slaves, constructed a house with Georgian, Greek Revival, and Italianate features, all popular styles in the antebellum period. The house took nearly a year to complete and was finally finished in May 1860. Tragically, though, William never had the chance to live in his new home. He died from yellow fever in April 1859—which is why some believe that it is his ghost that haunts the house today.

After the house was completed, Amanda and her seven children moved in. An enterprising woman, she, along with her sons and her brother, continued to run the family business, which included the store and sawmill, a gristmill, and one of the largest lumberyards in the region.

The Civil War brought death and ruin to many people in the state of Missouri, but thanks to the extension of personal credit to many people in the area, New Madrid managed to retain some semblance of normalcy during the war. Missouri was a divided state during the Civil War but the town was largely in favor of the Confederacy. One of the Hunter sons went off to serve in the Southern military during the conflict.

During two skirmishes in the area, known as the Battle of Island No. 10 and the Siege of New Madrid, the Hunter house and property were occupied by Union troops as they prepared to besiege the town. It is believed that the house was used as the headquarters of Gen. John Pope after the city was occupied by the Union. Somehow, though, the house and Hunter family survived the conflict relatively unscathed.

On Christmas Eve, 1874, the Hunters' youngest daughter, Ella, married William Dawson. After Amanda passed away in 1876, the house was left to Ella and William, who lived there until their deaths. While living in what became known as the Hunter-Dawson House, William served three terms in the Missouri State Legislature and in 1884 was elected to the U.S. House of Representatives. He also served on the planning committee for the 1893 Columbian Exposition in Chicago.

Descendants of the Hunter family continued living in the house until 1958. In 1966, it was purchased by the city of New Madrid and a year later, it was donated to the state to be used as a historic site. It remains open to the public today, reflecting the lifestyle of a successful antebellum businessman. Little seems to have changed here, as the house still contains many of the original furnishings and belongings from days long past. And many say it still contains one of the original occupants as well. Or at least he would have been an original occupant if he had lived long enough to see the house completed.

Stories have circulated about the Hunter-Dawson house since it became public property in the mid 1960s. Staff members, guides, and even visitors to the house have told stories of mysterious footsteps they have heard in empty rooms and hallways. Chairs that are placed in one section of the room when the house is closed for the night were often found in other locations the following day, often near a window as if someone were looking out onto the property. There are a number of reports from people who say they have seen the face of a man peering out the windows of the house as though he were looking for someone. When the house is checked for intruders, no one is ever found. Is this lonely face that of a ghost?

Some believe the wistful and restless ghost is none other than William Hunter, who carefully planned the house for his family and then died before he could live there. Is he still looking for the happiness that eluded him at the end of his life? Perhaps in his present existence, he has no idea how much time has passed and that his family will never return to the house they once loved. Perhaps he will continue to wait here in hopes that someday, the Hunter family will be reunited once more.

Ghosts of Cape Girardeau

Like many Missouri towns along the Mississippi River, Cape Girardeau was founded when there were few settlers in the western frontier regions of the country. It started as a temporary trading post in 1733, established by Jean Baptiste de Girardot, a French soldier from the Illinois settlement of Kaskaskia. The "cape" in the city's name is for a rock promontory overlooking the river, which was later destroyed by railroad construction. As early as 1765, this bend in the river was known as Cape Giradot, or Girardeau, but it would not become a full-fledged settlement until 1793, when the Spanish government gave Louis Lorimier the right to establish a trading post on a large tract of land that is now part of the town. Lorimier was made governor of the region and prospered from land sales and trading with the local Native Americans.

The town of Cape Girardeau was incorporated in 1808, prior to Missouri statehood, and was reincorporated as a city in 1843. The steamboat brought early prosperity to the city, and in the mid 1800s, it was the busiest port on the Mississippi between St. Louis and Memphis.

Like so many other Missouri towns, Cape Girardeau was bloodied by the Civil War. The Battle of Cape Girardeau took place on April 26, 1863, when Union and Confederate forces collided in a four-hour artillery barrage that claimed the lives of several dozen men.

As with any town that has a rich and storied past, history has left its mark on Cape Girardeau and that legacy makes itself known today through the local ghosts.

One of the most famous ghosts in town can be found at the Port Cape Girardeau Restaurant and Lounge, one of the oldest buildings in the city. It has anchored "Warehouse Row" on the riverfront since at least 1860 and has served as a commission house and warehouse over the years before becoming a restaurant. With the building's long history, it's no surprise that it has attracted a ghost.

A twenty-year veteran bartender at the place, Dale Pruett, nicknamed the resident spirit "Belle" because he got tired of calling her simply "the ghost." He came to believe the place was haunted after spending many nights alone in the building. He knew the old warehouse had many creaks and moans that were just a part of the aging structure, but he began hearing too many weird sounds that he couldn't explain.

He was willing to dismiss the strange sounds that seemed eerily like footsteps until one day something happened that he just couldn't laugh away. He was in a hallway downstairs and the bar area was empty. A nautical bell that was hung behind the bar suddenly began to ring. A hammer was kept next the bell, hanging from a leather strap, but no one had touched it. When Dale hurried into the bar, he saw that the room was empty. No one was there—no one that he could see, anyway—and he became convinced at that moment that the place was truly haunted.

There are a few stories of how the ghost of "Belle" came to reside at the warehouse, but no one knows if any of them are accurate. Each story tells of a Union soldier who abandons a woman who believed she would become his bride. In despair, the woman commits suicide; in most variations of the legend, she throws herself from an upper window of the warehouse. Over time, so many people have encountered the spirit that she has become a part of the restaurant's history.

And she refuses to remain silent—or invisible.

Unusual noises—unusual even for a building a century and a half old—are not uncommon at Port Cape Girardeau and neither are the disembodied footsteps that tap back and forth in deserted rooms and upstairs hallways. A number of people, including Dale Pruett, have felt Belle's hand touch them on the back or shoulder. When they turn to see who is trying to get their attention, there is never anyone there. Sightings of the ghost are few and far between, but they do happen. Over the years, Pruett has collected more than a handful of matching descriptions of a shadowy woman in a long dress. Sometimes, he believes, she just wants to get people's attention.

If you're visiting Cape Girardeau and looking for a place where you can wine and dine with the spirits, looked no further than this old place on Warehouse Row. You just might come face to face with a little part of the building's past.

The most legendary—and eerie—location in Cape Girardeau is the Old Lorimier Cemetery. Listed in the National Register of Historic Places, and the burial place of more than twelve hundred Civil War soldiers as well as the city's founder, Louis Lorimier, the cemetery dates back to the earliest days of Cape Girardeau.

Created on land that was granted to the city by Lorimier, the site is believed to hold more than six thousand graves, although hundreds of them are unmarked. The first burial that took place was that of Lorimier's wife, Charlotte, a Native American woman. She was buried on a hilltop in 1808 and the rest of the graveyard grew up around her resting place, eventually forming in an unusual way. The Old Lorimier Cemetery is cut into two sections by a walkway. It is believed that this walkway served as a marker to where the dead could be interred. The north side was said to belong to the Protestants, while Catholics were buried on the south side.

Thanks to the age of the cemetery and the long shadow of legend that has been cast over the grounds, it's not surprising that a number of ghost stories have become associated with the place over the years. The most persistent story of the burial ground is that of the "Tapping Ghost."

For more than a century, there was no fence around Old Lorimier Cemetery and it was easy for people to walk through the graveyard at all times of the day and night. People who lived on the side of town that was north of the cemetery would often cut through the grounds on their way to the downtown business district. No one thought anything strange about this, even in the dead of night, until the stories of the Tapping Ghost began making the rounds in the early 1900s.

According to the stories, people who passed through the cemetery after dark would often feel someone tap them on the shoulder as they walked. They turned to see who had so silently approached them, but no one was ever there. Assuming that it was their imaginations, or perhaps something falling from a tree, they dismissed the disturbance and walked on. A few moments later, though, the tapping came again, much more persistent this time. Frightened, they hurried out the cemetery and, when downtown, told people of their experience. The stories became so widely reported that reporters even noted new encounters with the Tapping Ghost in the local newspaper.

But the ghosts of Old Lorimier Cemetery don't confine themselves to just tapping people on the shoulder. There have also been many accounts of people, mostly women, who have been walking through the cemetery and have had someone—or something—tug their hair from behind. Some of the stories say that these tugs have been hard enough to bring tears to the eyes of the victims. It seems clear that some of the spirits that linger in the graveyard are desperate to get someone's attention!

One of the most talked-about legends of Old Lorimier Cemetery is that of the alleged tunnel that runs from the graveyard to the Sherwood-Minton House, located just a block away. The house was used as a smallpox hospital during the Civil War and it was said that soldiers who died there were transported through the tunnel to the cemetery so as to avoid panic among the townspeople over the possible spread of the sickness. Most have scoffed at the idea that the tunnel ever existed; no record or trace of the tunnel has ever been found. However, there are stories dating back to the years just after the war that do hint of a ghostly connection between the house and the graveyard.

The deed to the Sherwood-Minton house dates back to the early 1800s, when it was part of the land that belonged to Louis Lorimier. After Lorimier's death, the estate was settled and the land was purchased by Charles Ellis in 1819. His son, Alfred, sold twenty acres of the land to the Reverend and Mrs. Adiel Sherwood, who built the grand house on the property. Reverend Sherwood hired architect E.B. Deane to design the house. Most of the lumber was cut on the property and all of the glass and bricks were handmade.

In 1849, the Washington Female Seminary moved into the Sherwood home. The Reverend David Edward Young Rice was the first principal and the cost for boarding students was $65 for a five-month session with an additional $1 that went toward heating the classrooms. The seminary remained in the building until 1971.

During the Civil War, though, the school was first used to house soldiers, and then was turned into a military smallpox hospital. It is from this time period that the stories of the tunnel and the ghosts have emerged.

There were many stories told about the house and its ghostly guests, which are mostly believed to be the spirits of soldiers who died there when it was a hospital. These stories began to be told just after the end of the war, as evidenced by an article that appeared in a 1910 edition of the *Missouri Republican* newspaper. The article appeared on June 29 and mostly concerned the collapse of one of the north walls of the Sherwood House. However, accompanying the main article was a short piece that mentioned that the house was alleged to be haunted and recounted an incident from 1867. It read:

> The appearance of ghostly visitors at frequent intervals made the house an undesirable one for a home. Many nights the tall, white form of a departed soldier was seen moving about through the trees of the park surrounding the house, either disappearing into the ground, into the abandoned house or fading into the darkness of the somber grove of the park, The ownership of the house passed into the hands of a family named Morris, whose heirs had become scattered throughout the union; it therefore stood untenanted and uncared for, and the fact that it was haunted by the spirits of soldiers dead and gone made it all the more undesirable for a home.
>
> Members of the Justi post, G.A.R., hearing of the visits of the ghostly soldiers, decided to make an investigation, a committee was appointed and a watch was set. The members of the committee concealed themselves in the shrubbery about the place one night in June in the year 1867, and began their watch for the coming of the restless spirit. As the clocks about the village were striking the midnight hour, they saw a sight which caused their hearts, although they were the hearts of veteran soldiers, to thump within their breasts. From the cemetery across the way there glided toward them a tall specter, white clad, moving silently and slowly among the trees. Nearer it came, the faint moonlight giving it an uncanny appearance. The three men

crouching breathlessly behind the shrubbery were almost spell-bound with awe as the specter glided toward them, and in all probability would have fled, but that the ghost, unfortunately for himself, and probably owing to the dampness of the night air, was so un-ghostly as to sneeze.

That sneeze was the undoing of his ghostship, for it broke the spell which had held the watchers in check. A dash was made, and a few minutes later the ghost was flat on his back, and the familiar features of Philoh Smith, a well-known contractor and builder of Cape Girardeau, were lying uncovered in the light of the moon, which had come merrily out from behind the clouds. Philoh Smith, who owned adjoining property, had long desired to acquire the Sherwood place, and had resorted to the ghostly method of beating down the purchase price.

Did this mean that the Sherwood House was not haunted? Perhaps—or perhaps not, since the stories of phantom soldiers were around before the hijinks of Philoh Smith and have lingered in legend ever since. Those spectral soldiers were not only seen at the house but also at the nearby cemetery. In addition to the probably mythical tunnel, soldiers quartered at the hospital were said to have transported the dead in processions to the burial ground under the cover of darkness and buried them in secret. These grim processions have allegedly repeated themselves over the years as phantom funerals, often seen in the early-morning hours as ghostly figures carrying the bodies of the deceased on their shoulders to a silent grave.

Cape Girardeau is a place where the past literally comes alive and refuses to be forgotten.

Down
in the Ozarks

Wilson's Creek Battlefield

The Battle of Wilson's Creek, also known as the Battle of Oak Hills, was fought on August 10, 1861, near Springfield, between Union troops and the Missouri State Guard. While considered by historians the first major battle of the Civil War fought west of the Mississippi—it's sometimes referred to as the "Bull Run of the West"—it's often forgotten by those who believe the war was fought only on the battlefields of the East.

The hours of bloody fighting that occurred at this lonely spot left an indelible impression on the landscape of southwest Missouri and tales of hauntings still reverberate more than 150 years after the last shots were fired on the battlefield.

At the start of the Civil War, Missouri declared that it would be an "armed neutral" state in the conflict and not send men or materials to either side. However, that neutrality was quickly put to test on May 10, 1861, by Governor Claiborne F. Jackson, who leaned toward the Confederate cause. He had called out the state militia to drill on the edge of pro-Union St. Louis and after secretly obtaining artillery from the Confederacy, smuggled it into the militia camp at Lindell Grove that came to be known as "Camp

Jackson." Federal captain Nathaniel Lyon was aware of the guns and feared that the militia was planning to attack the St. Louis arsenal. Thomas W. Sweeny was put in command of the arsenal's defense, and Lyon surrounded the militia camp with Union troops and home guards, forcing the surrender of the militia. He blundered, though, when he marched the captured militia through the streets, attracting crowds, many of whom were angry and pressed against the procession. Taunts and fighting eventually led to gunfire and many civilian and military deaths.

The following day, the violence in St. Louis led the Missouri General Assembly to create the Missouri State Guard, which was tasked with defending the state from attacks by perceived enemies, from either the North or the South. The governor appointed Sterling Price as the commander with the rank of major general. The State Guard was organized into divisions, with each division consisting of units raised from a military district of Missouri and command by a brigadier general.

Fearing that Missouri would fall to the Confederacy, William S. Harney, Missouri's Federal commander, struck the Price-Harney Truce on May 12, 1861, which affirmed the state's neutrality. Governor Jackson then declared his support for the Union. However, Harney was replaced with Nathaniel Lyon, now promoted to brigadier general, and Abraham Lincoln made a specific request for Missouri troops to enter into Federal service. With that, Jackson withdrew his support. On June 12, Lyon and Jackson met in St. Louis with hopes of resolving the matter, but things went badly. The meeting ended with Lyon's now iconic words, "This means war. In an hour, one of my officers will call for you and conduct you out of my lines."

Lyon sent a force under General Sweeney to Springfield while his own forces captured the state capital and pursued Jackson, Price, and the now-exiled state government across Missouri. Skirmishes occurred at Boonville and Carthage. In light of the crisis, the delegates of the Missouri Constitutional Convention that had rejected secession in February convened again. On July 27, the convention declared the governor's office vacant and selected Hamilton Rowan Gamble to be the new provisional governor.

By July 13, Lyon's army of about six thousand men was encamped at Springfield. His force was composed of the 1st, 2nd,

3rd, and 5th Missouri Infantry, the 1st Iowa Infantry, the 1st Kansas and 2nd Kansas Infantry, several companies of Regular Army infantry and cavalry, and three batteries of artillery. He divided the units into four brigades commanded by Maj. Samuel D. Sturgis, Col. Franz Sigel, Lt. Col. George Andrews, and Col. George Dietzler.

By the end of July, the Missouri State Guard was encamped about seventy-five miles southwest of Springfield and had been reinforced by Confederate brigadier general Benjamin McCulloch and Arkansas state militia brigadier general N. Bart Pearce. The now mixed Missouri and Confederate forces were double the size of Lyon's Union force. They began making plans to attack Springfield but on August 1, Lyon marched out of the city in a bold move to try and surprise the Confederate forces. A short skirmish occurred at Dug Springs, with the Union emerging as the winner, but by then Lyon had learned that he was greatly outnumbered by the enemy and retreated back into Springfield. McCulloch went in pursuit and by August 6 was encamped at Wilson's Creek, about ten miles southwest of the city.

The pursuit was slowed by bickering between Price and McCulloch. Price favored an immediate attack on Springfield but McCulloch, doubtful about the quality of the Missouri State Guard, preferred to remain in place. After Price threatened an attack without his support, McCulloch reluctantly agreed to attack on the morning of August 10, only to be stopped by a heavy rainstorm on the night of August 9. He canceled his plans and ordered his men back to camp.

Meanwhile, Lyon knew that his smaller force was in great danger. He began making plans to withdraw northeast to Rolla where he could reinforce and resupply—but not before he launched a surprise attack on the Missouri camp to slow the enemy's pursuit. Colonel Sigel developed a flawed strategy, with which Lyon unfortunately agreed, that split the already outnumbered Union force. Sigel proposed trapping McCulloch with a pincer movement. He would lead twelve hundred men in a flanking maneuver while the main body of troops under Lyon struck from the north. Going along with the ill-conceived plan, the Union troops marched out of Springfield on the dark, wet night of August 9, leaving behind about one thousand men to protect the supplies and cover the retreat.

The Union force attacked at first light on August 10. The Confederates were taken by surprise and Lyon's force overran their camps and took the high ground at the crest of a ridge that came to be known as "Bloody Hill." But the Union's hopes for a quick victory were dashed when the artillery of the Pulaski Arkansas Battery opened up on their advance, which gave Price's infantry time to organize lines on the south side of the hill. Lyon attempted to counterattack from his position but was unsuccessful. Price launched a series of frontal and flank attacks against Lyon but was also unsuccessful. Eventually, a shortage of ammunition caused Price's attack to falter.

The two Union forces, commanded by Lyon and Sigel, lost contact with each other since they had no means of communicating and no way of supporting each other if anything went wrong. Sigel's attack was successful at first, with the brigade arriving in the Confederate rear just as the sun was coming up. Artillery fire routed the Confederate cavalry units that were encamped at the Sharp Farm and Sigel started a pursuit that stopped along Skegg's Branch. When he inexplicably stopped at this position, he failed to post skirmishers along his front and left his flank open for an attack. Meanwhile, McCulloch rallied several Confederate units, including the 3rd Louisiana Infantry and the 3rd Division from the Missouri State Guard, and launched a counterattack. Sigel's men mistook the 3rd Louisiana for the 3rd Iowa Infantry, who also wore gray uniforms, and withheld their fire until the Confederates were nearly upon them. Sigel's flank was consequently devastated by the counterattack and his brigade was routed, losing four cannons. Sigel and his men fled the field and Lyon, Sweeny, and Sturgis were left on the field alone.

After Sigel was driven from the battle, the momentum shifted in favor of the Confederacy. Nathaniel Lyon became the first Union general to be killed in the war. He was shot in the heart at Bloody Hill, at about 9:30 A.M., while leading the 2nd Kansas Infantry in a countercharge. General Sweeny was shot in the leg, and Major Sturgis, as the highest-ranking Regular Army officer, assumed command of the troops. By this time, the Federal men were still in a defensible position atop the hill, but supplies were low and morale was worsening by the minute. By 11:00 A.M., the Union troops had repulsed three separate Confederate charges.

Finally, fearing a fourth Confederate attack, Sturgis retreated and the Federals fled toward Rolla.

In the aftermath of the bloody battle, the casualties were nearly equal—1,317 Union and 1,230 from the Missouri, Arkansas, and Confederate troops. Though the Confederates won the day, they were unable to pursue the retreating Union forces. Once again, Price and McCulloch argued. Price wanted to start immediately in pursuit but McCulloch feared for the condition of the troops and didn't want to stretch the supply line from Arkansas any farther than he had to. The Confederate and Arkansas forces eventually withdrew from the state.

After falling back to Springfield, Sturgis handed over command of the army to Sigel. At a council of war that evening, it was agreed that the Federal troops would fall back to Rolla. However, Sigel failed to get his brigade ready on time, forcing a delay of several hours. Along the retreat route, Sigel's men took several lengthy delays in order to prepare meals; eventually, the other officers turned on Sigel and forced him to turn command back over to Sturgis. Throughout the rest of the war, Sigel largely failed to distinguish himself, often blaming poor health for bad decisions and defeats. He was soundly defeated by Maj. Gen. John C. Breckenridge's troops at the Battle of New Market, Virginia, on May 15, 1864, which was particularly embarrassing due to the prominent role young cadets from the Virginia Military Institute played in his defeat. In July 1864, Sigel fought Lt. Gen. Jubal A. Early at Harpers Ferry, West Virginia, but soon afterward was relieved of his command for "lack of aggression." Sigel spent the rest of the war without an active command.

The Battle of Wilson's Creek was an important moment for the Confederate sympathizers in southwest Missouri. On October 30, 1861, the Missourians under Price and Jackson formally joined the Confederate cause in Neosho, Missouri. Officials passed the resolutions for Missouri secession and Jackson was named the Governor of Confederate Missouri. However, the new government never earned the favor of most of the population of Missouri, and the state remained officially in the Union throughout the war. To make matters worse, a series of defeats shattered what little control Jackson had and his Confederate state government was soon forced to leave Missouri.

War had shattered the peace of rural Missouri and it would be many years before the violence and bloodshed would come to an end.

One hundred years after the last guns were silenced at Wilson's Creek, the battlefield was designated a national park. Today, travelers and history buffs visit this quiet park, which is filled with trees and prairie grass and looks almost the same as it did in 1861. The stories of bravery and blood seem far in the past in this peaceful place—but they may not be as distant as one might think.

One of the ghosts lingering at Wilson's Creek may not be linked directly to the battle. The John Ray House, which was in the midst of the fighting in 1861, was built in 1850 and was the Wilson's Creek post office for more than ten years. It was home to Ray, his wife, Roxana, their nine children, and a mail carrier. The house was occupied by Confederate officers during the battle.

The Ray family has been gone for many years, but at least one member of the family may have stayed behind. On several occasions, visitors have seen a young woman in a long period dress carrying water from the Ray springhouse, a small stone building that covered a nearby spring. The family stored perishables like milk, butter, and eggs in the springhouse and used the water for drinking and cooking. Those who have seen the girl believed that she was part of a living-history program at the battlefield, but when they tried to speak to her, she didn't respond. Park rangers stated that there was no living-history program going on at the time of the sightings.

Most of the ghostly occurrences at Wilson's Creek, however, take place on the battlefield itself, where more than 2,000 young men were killed or wounded in August 1861. Battlefields, with all of the trauma and death that occurred on them, are common places to find ghosts and hauntings, and Wilson's Creek is no exception.

Stories about ghosts on the site date back at least as far as the 1940s, when a group of fisherman saw at least fifteen Union soldiers, wearing dirty uniforms and carrying rifles. The soldiers filed past them and vanished. The same group of spectral soldiers has been seen several times near the creek. It was as if a supernatural recording imprinted itself on the location and now repeats itself over and over again.

Civil War reenactor Steve Cottrell told of an incident that occurred in the spring of 1983, when the park sponsored a large encampment of reenactors to present military drills, camp life, and battle re-creations for visitors. During that weekend, a column of Union infantry reenactors went on an early-morning march. In the predawn light, the men became aware of a solitary horseman who was following them at a distance. Although his features were not clear, he was dressed in Civil War clothing. By the time the march was over, the lone figure on horseback had disappeared. The men assumed that the rider was a cavalry reenactor out on a morning ride. However, when the men in the cavalry unit (including Cottrell) heard about the incident, they were surprised because none of the men had been riding at that time of the morning. As far as they were able to determine, no one—reenactor, visitor, or park ranger—was on horseback in the park at the time the lone rider made his appearance.

There is no place on the battlefield more haunted than Bloody Hill, the site of numerous deaths during the fight. Union batteries on the hilltop dueled with Confederate artillery in the valley for more than six hours and the Federal men on high ground fought off three charges by the desperate Missouri and Arkansas men who threw themselves at the line over and over again. Hundreds of men died both attacking and defending the hill and, not surprisingly, some of them have remained behind.

Over the years, many people who have visited Bloody Hill have spoken of feeling as if they were not alone on the hilltop. And while this could be blamed on the imaginations of those who knew of the violent events on the hill, other incidents suggest that there is more here than meets the eye. Accounts have circulated of voices, cries, shouts, and screams that have been heard there, even when no living person was nearby. Some claim to have actually seen the mournful apparitions of torn and bloody soldiers on the hill, often sending these unlucky visitors hurrying back to their cars.

There is little doubt among those who have encountered the unusual out in the trees and prairie grass of the park that something remains at Wilson's Creek.

Peace Church Cemetery

Peace Church Cemetery is an old, ramshackle, and mostly abandoned burial ground near Joplin. Over the years, reports have circulated about strange sounds, voices, and eerie lights that have been heard and seen in the cemetery. There are also reports of a ghostly figure that has been seen lurking in the trees, peering out at passersby and then vanishing when approached. It would be safe to assume that one of the restless souls buried here does not rest in peace. And when you learn just who is buried in this cemetery, in a forsaken, unmarked grave, a likely identity for this restless spirit emerges.

Few mass murderers have ever gone on a worse killing spree than the one twenty-one-year-old Billy Cook started on December 30, 1950. On that day, Cook, posing as a hitchhiker, forced a motorist at gunpoint to get into the trunk of his own car and then drove away. Over the next two weeks, Cook went on a senseless rampage. He kidnapped nearly a dozen people, including a deputy sheriff, and murdered six of them in cold blood, including three children. He also attempted other killings and terrorized the southwestern border states.

Cook was born in 1929 and grew up near Joplin. His early life was hard. His father was an uneducated mine worker who, after the death of Cook's mother, raised Billy and his seven brothers and sisters in an abandoned mine shaft. One night, after drinking in a local tavern, he hopped a freight train and left the children to survive alone. Authorities found them huddled in the old mine, living like animals. Welfare workers were able to find foster homes for all of the children, except for Billy. His attitude caused people to stay away from him and he had a sinister-looking affliction of the right eye that would not allow the lid to close all the way. He was finally taken in by a woman who did it purely for the money paid to her by the government; she and the boy never got along.

As he got older, Billy stayed out at night, getting in trouble, and he ended up spending most of his formative years in reform school. He told a judge that he would prefer it to foster care and he got his wish. He was simply born bad, most believed. When he was young, Billy had the words "Hard Luck" tattooed across the knuckles of both of his hands.

After being released from reform school, Cook immediately robbed a cab driver of $11 and stole a car. He was soon caught and sent back to reform school for five years. He became one of the most dangerous inmates in the institution and was sent to the Missouri Penitentiary to finish his sentence. While there, he beat another inmate so badly with a baseball bat that the man almost died. The victim had made the mistake of laughing at Cook's drooping eyelid.

In 1950, Cook was released and returned to Joplin to look for his father. The reunion was short-lived. Billy left town and started hitching rides through the Southwest, ending up in Blythe, California. There he got only job that he ever held, washing dishes in a diner, but he soon grew bored and began to roam again, this time heading for Texas. Somewhere along the way, he picked up a snub-nosed .32-caliber pistol and he kept it tucked away in his pocket. Cook had little use for anyone; he hated people—all people—and he decided to put those feelings into action when he kidnapped his first victim, a motorist he encountered near Lubbock, Texas. Cook locked him in the trunk of his own car but the driver managed to use a jack handle to open the trunk from the inside. He held the trunk closed until Cook turned off the highway and onto a secondary road. Convinced that Cook planned to kill him, the man jumped out when the car slowed down and escaped by running across the flatland.

Cook drove the lonely stretch of highway between Claremore and Tulsa, Oklahoma, before the stolen car ran out of gas. He left the vehicle on the side of the road and walked on. A few minutes later, he saw a 1949 Chevrolet coming toward him. Cook waved frantically, as if he had encountered car problems, in an effort to get the car to slow down.

The driver, Carl Mosser, brought the car to a stop. Mosser, his wife Thelma, and their three small children were on vacation from Decatur, Illinois, on their way to New Mexico. They picked up Cook alongside the road. Many today would wonder why they picked up a hitchhiker with small children in the car but those were different times; Americans had not yet been bombarded with the gruesome images of death and murder that were to come in the media and in entertainment. They had nothing to fear, they believed, and simply wanted to help out a young man who was down on his luck. Cook repaid the family's kindness by pulling a gun and forcing Mosser to drive into Oklahoma and then to Texas. Carl Mosser, frantically worried for his family, hoped that his twin brother, Chris, who lived in Albuquerque and was expecting the family for a visit, would start to worry and alert the authorities.

Cook forced him to drive to Wichita Falls, Texas, and Mosser desperately kept thinking of ways to try and get rid of the maniac. He thought he saw a chance in Wichita Falls when the car started to run low on gas. He urged Cook into a filling station for some fuel and food. Mosser pulled into the station and told the elderly attendant to fill the tank. When he asked, at Cook's orders, that some lunch meat be brought to the car, the attendant told him that he would have to get that himself. Mosser went inside, followed by Cook, and it was then that Mosser grabbed Cook and tried to pin him from behind. Frightened, the attendant pulled an old revolver and waved it nervously at the two struggling men. He ordered Mosser to let loose of Cook and Carl tried to explain what was happening. Too scared to help, the old man ordered them out of the station. The two continued to fight until Cook broke away and pushed Mosser through a plate-glass window.

The old man, now terrified, locked himself inside as Cook ordered Mosser back to the car. As the automobile drove off, the old man jumped into his truck and gave chase. Cook saw him coming and fired several shots at him. With that, the attendant's bravery vanished and he stopped the truck.

Cook was now seething with anger and he forced Mosser to drive to Carlsbad, New Mexico, and then on to El Paso, Texas. From there, the terrifying journey continued to Houston and then on to Winthrop, Arkansas. Cook then had Mosser turn the car toward his old stomping grounds in Joplin. Finally, more than seventy-two hours after the family was kidnapped, Thelma Mosser became hysterical and started to cry. The children also began to wail and Cook gagged all of them except for Carl. Soon, when a police officer seemed to be paying too much attention to the Mosser car, Cook grew tired of his game and turned his pistol on the family. He shot and killed all of them and for good measure, shot the family dog, too. He dumped their bodies in a place he knew well: an abandoned mine shaft near Joplin.

Eventually, the Mossers' car was found abandoned near Tulsa, Oklahoma. It looked like a slaughter pen, with the upholstery ripped by bullets and blood splashed everywhere. The victims' bodies were soon discovered, as well as an important clue Cook had left behind in the car: the receipt for the handgun that he had bought. His identity was soon learned and a massive manhunt was launched.

Cook headed for California, where he kidnapped a deputy sheriff who had almost captured him. He forced the deputy to drive him around while he bragged about executing the Mosser family. After more than forty miles, Cook ordered the lawman to stop and forced him to lie down in a ditch with his hands tied behind his back. He told the man that he was going to put a bullet in his head, but then, for some reason, he climbed into the car and drove away. The officer waited for the bullet but it never came. He would never know why he was spared. A short time later, Cook flagged down another motorist, Robert Dewey, and wounded him. The two men struggled and the car left the road and careened out into the desert. Cook ended the fight with a bullet to Dewey's head and he threw the body into a ditch.

By this time, an alarm had been raised all over the Southwest and so Cook decided to head into Mexico. He kidnapped two men and brought them along to Santa Rosalia, a number of miles across the border. Amazingly, though, Cook was recognized by the local police chief, Francisco Morales. He simply walked up to Cook, snatched the gun from the man's belt, and placed him under arrest. Cook was then rushed to the border and turned over to FBI agents.

Despite the slaying of the Mosser family, the Justice Department turned Cook over to the California courts and he was tried for the murder of Robert Dewey. Cook displayed as much regret about this murder as about the others—in other words, none—and he was sentenced to death. On December 12, 1952, he died in the gas chamber at San Quentin.

After his death, Billy's body was brought back to Missouri. After first being laid out for viewing in Comanche, Oklahoma—a ritual that brought out more than 12,000 curiosity-seekers—he was buried in the dark of night at Peace Church Cemetery. According to a 1952 *Joplin Globe* article, a brief service was held

by flashlight and lantern light, with about fifteen people in atten-
dance. Just as the grave service ended, a reporter wrote, "the cry
of a small child could be heard in the chill of the night air."

Billy Cook was laid to rest in an unmarked grave but most
believe that he does not rest quietly at the edge of the old graveyard. Throughout the years, stories have circulated about the
shadowy figure that has been seen lurking about on the grounds
and wandering among the nearby trees. Whoever this man is, he
seems lost and confused and some have remarked that he appears
to be angry about something.

If this lingering spirit is that of Billy Cook, then his anger
becomes clear. As in life, Cook hated everyone and everything,
and it's likely that his hatred hasn't cooled, even in death.

In Search of the Hornet Spook Light

Spook lights, or ghost lights as they are often called, have long
been a part of anomalous history in America. Such a light is best
defined as being a luminous phenomenon that, because of regular manifestation, the way that it behaves, and its location, is put
into a separate category from ball lightning or such supernatural
phenomena as ghosts. However, most spook lights, especially
those that appear regularly over a period of time in one location,
tend to take on a supernatural air. Legends tend to grow around
them, concerning strange deaths and most often a beheading with
a ghost returning to look for its severed head. The spook light is
most often said to be the light of a lantern that the spirit carries
to assist him in the search.

Spook lights appear in hundreds of places around the country.
While most of them have an eerie legend or two attached to them,
there are few explanations for them. In the instances when the
lights have been thoroughly investigated, the results have been
inconclusive at best and disappointing at worst. In some cases,
the mysterious lights turn out to be nothing more than the headlights of cars on distant highways or reflections of stars refracted
though layers of different air temperatures. But that's not always
the case.

There are a number of locations where spook lights appear
that cannot be accounted for with such explanations. These are

places where reports of the lights date back to well before the advent of the automobile and where claims of artificial lights in the distance just don't hold up. These are lights that serious researchers have been unable to debunk. And while it is the opinion of many with an interest in such things that spook lights are a natural part of our world for which we do not yet have an explanation, the most compelling ones still remain unsolved.

Located about twenty miles or so southwest of Joplin is a roughly paved road where one of America's favorite spook lights puts in a regular appearance. This old and otherwise forgotten track runs across the Oklahoma border and is only about four miles long. Nearby is the border village of Hornet and close to that is the site of what once was a spook light museum. The place is remote and far from civilization, so why do so many people come here?

They are searching for an unexplained enigma, a puzzle that many of them find. It has been seen along this road since 1866 and has created such a mystery that even the Army Corps of Engineers officially concluded that it was a "mysterious light of unknown origin." It has been called by many names since it started appearing near what is called the Devil's Promenade, but it's most commonly known as the Hornet Spook Light.

This light has appeared, looking like a ball of fire, for nearly a century and a half, varying from the size of a softball to larger. It spins down the center of this gravel road at great speed, rises up high, and bobs and weaves to the right and left. It appears to be a large lantern, but there is never anyone carrying it. The light has also appeared inside vehicles. It seems to retreat when it is pursued and never allows anyone to get to close to it. Does it have some sort of intelligence? This remains just one of the many mysteries connected to this light.

No one has ever been injured by the light but many have been frightened by it while walking or driving down this road at night. Sometimes it seems to come from nowhere, and a few witnesses claim they have felt the heat from it as it passed close to them. Occasionally, some observer will even take a shot or two at the light, like Franklin Rossman, who lived near the Devil's Promenade for years. He twice attempted to shoot the light with a hunting rifle but the shots had no effect on it whatsoever. He told a spook light investigator that he was unable to judge the distance to the light because it had such an odd look to it. When asked what he meant by this, Rossman was unable to explain. It just looked "sort of blurry," he said.

Many theories have attempted to explain why this mysterious light appears here. One of the early legends claimed the light was connected to the spirit of two young Quapaw Indians who died in the area many years ago. Another claimed the light was the spirit of an Osage Indian chief who had been beheaded on the Devil's Promenade; the light was said to be his torch as he searched for his missing head. Another legend tells of a farmer whose children were kidnapped by Indians. He set off looking for them with only a lantern to light his way. The mysterious light is said to be that very lantern as the farmer's ghost continues looking for the children that he will never find.

Locals claim that the stories of the Hornet Light started back in the 1800s, but most printed accounts are of a much more recent vintage. As far as is known, the first account of it appeared in the *Kansas City Star* in 1936 and then in the 1947 book *Ozark Superstitions* by Vance Randolph, the famed Missouri folklorist. Randolph was the first to put into print the oral legends of the light's origins, from beheaded Indians to lost children.

In 1958, a writer for the *Ford Times* investigated the light and described it as a diffused orange glow that floated and weaved along the roadway. He also noted that it seemed to change size as he watched it, varying between the size of apple and that of a bushel basket. He also saw the light split off into three different lights and then merge into a single light, as it settled down upon the branch of a tree and changed colors from orange to blue.

Over the years, the light has been studied, researched, chased, photographed, and shot at—but what is it? While legends give one reason for the light, its genuine origins seem to present a formidable problem. Many suggestions have been offered as to what could cause the light to appear; for many years the most popular theory was that it was merely a will-o'-the-wisp, the name given to a biological phenomenon that is caused by the decay of wood and organic materials. The light that comes from the decay is often bright and can be seen on occasion in wooded areas and damp regions. As fascinating as this is, it really doesn't explain the Hornet Light. Instances of will-o'-the-wisp simply do not give off the intensity of light that has been reported along the Devil's Promenade.

Another suggestion has been the ever-popular "marsh gas." Unfortunately, while an abundance of marsh gas in a marsh or swamp would certainly be flammable, it cannot spontaneously light itself. Even if it did, wind and rain would soon extinguish any flame that appeared. Strong winds that have been reported during sightings of the Hornet Light do not seem to disturb the light, and they don't keep it from moving in whatever direction it pleases.

There have also been suggestions that the light might be a glow coming from minerals in the area. This seems doubtful, too, as the light does not always appear in the same place. One theory is that the light might be formed by electrical fields in areas where earthquakes and ground shifts take place. This is a possibility, since there are fault lines in the region. Four large earthquakes took place in the area in the early 1800s that had a devastating effect on this part of the state. It is possible that the lights started to appear around the time of the earthquakes but were not reported until the population in the area started to grow around the time of the Civil War.

Other "experts" claim they have the mystery solved and that it's not unexplainable at all. They claim the light is caused by automobiles driving on the highway about five miles east of what's known as "Spook Light Road." They say the highway is on a direct line with it but at a slightly lower elevation. When it is pointed out that a high ridge separates the area from the highway, the experts explain how refraction causes light to bend and creates the eerie effect that so many people have reported as the spook light.

Believe it or not, several investigations that have been conducted at the site have shown that some of the sightings can be attributed to this. Dr. George W. Ward, formerly of the Bureau of Standards in Washington, D.C., and later with the Midwest Research Institute, investigated the light in 1945. He said that shortly after arriving at the site, he saw a diffused glow appear over some low hills. A few moments later, a sphere of light appeared that looked to be four to six feet in diameter. Ward humorously added that the publicity director of the Midwest Institute remarked to the others assembled that he had seen all that he cared to and as the light approached the group, he quickly locked himself inside their car.

But Ward was critical about the source of the light. During his study, he decided that the light must originate to the west of the viewing site and over the range of hills in the distance. He surmised that the refraction of auto headlights from a road that was in line with the country lane could create an illusion of a traveling light. Dr. Ward checked his maps and found that such a road did exist, a section of highway that ran east-west between Commerce and Quapaw, Oklahoma. He suggested that an airplane might be used to spot cars on the highway and relay the information to observers at the Spook Light site. If the lights could be shown to correspond with the Hornet light, the mystery would be solved.

Captain Bob E. Loftin followed up on these speculations with his own experiments a few years later. He discovered that colored test lights that were placed on the suspected areas of Route 66 could be seen from Spook Light Road. He further reasoned that moving cars along the highway would appear as spheres of light, closely grouped together. He also added that changing humidity and temperature would cause the lights that were created to behave strangely. This, he reasoned, would explain the number of unusual stories told about the way the light acted.

And while this would admittedly explain some of the sightings of the Hornet Light, it is impossible that it could explain them all. The most important point to remember is that the light was being seen before the invention of automobiles.

These were far from the only investigations conducted at the site. Author Raymond Bayless embarked on an extensive study of the spook light in October 1963. Around dusk on the evening of October 17, he and several assistants spotted the light for the first time, when it appeared as a bright light some distance along the roadway. He reported that the light fluctuated in intensity and at times became two separate lights, hovering one above the other. The light returned again about an hour later and according to Bayless, was so bright that it caused a reflection on the dirt surface of the road. A few minutes after the light appeared, the investigation group began moving westward along the road in pursuit of it. The light receded backward (or appeared to) as they got closer to it. The group began navigating the hills and ravines of the road and the light vanished. It did not reappear until they reached a point near the old spook light museum, which was still in operation at that time.

The "Spooksville Museum," then operated by Leslie W. Robertson, offered not only photographs and a collection of accounts about the light but also a viewing platform for people to observe the light with the naked eye or through telescopes and cameras. A member of Bayless's group set up a small refracting telescope on the platform and they were able to learn that what appeared to be a single light was actually composed of a number of smaller lights. Bayless stated that they moved very close together, weaving slightly, expanding and contracting back and forth. The lights were amber and gold in color and sometimes gained a reddish tint for a few moments at a time. Through the telescope, the edges of the light were observed to be like a "flame" in that they were not uniform and constantly changed.

Bayless was fascinated with the many explanations given for the light and was able to rule out almost all of the ones that had been proposed, including the theory that all of the sightings could be explained away as the refraction of auto headlights. In fact, Arthur Holbrook, a resident of the area and a man who had investigated the light many times, told Bayless that he had first seen the light in 1905. At that time, Holbrook explained, there were only about a dozen automobiles in Joplin, the closest large town. He also added that there had been no highways at that period and because of this, headlights could not have explained his sightings of the light. The few cars that were in existence in the area at that time did not travel on remote, dirt lanes that were best suited for horses, and any autos that would have traveled around the region were only fitted with oil and carbide lamps, which would not have been capable of creating the long, intense beams that modern headlights emit. To add even more credibility to his account, Holbrook was in the automotive profession and would have been very aware of the number of autos in the region in those days and the state of the roads and highways.

But did the light actually exist before automobiles came to southwest Missouri or was this merely a part of the local legend? Many skeptics claimed that the enigma's longevity was simply a facet of the light's folklore but Bayless did not agree. After conducting a number of interviews in the area, he began to believe that the light had been seen in the 1800s. He did not feel that his own sighting of the light was due to auto headlights, but as it had been shown that some lights would appear on the road as refraction from the highway, he needed to gather as much evidence as possible to show that the light predated automobiles. Holbrook had experienced his first sighting of the light in 1905 and had heard of the light for several years before that. After that first sighting, he rode out in a buggy to see the light many times and told Bayless that the light was the same in the 1960s as it had been in 1905.

Bayless also interviewed Leslie Robertson, the curator of the Spooksville Museum, who first saw the light in 1916. He was only fourteen years old at the time and during his lifetime he had seen the light literally "thousands of times."

John Muening of Joplin first saw the light around 1928 and had heard stories about it for a number of years before that. He told Bayless that "we have watched it all night . . . Highway 66 has nothing to do with the light. It couldn't have, as it didn't exist when the light was first seen, of that I am sure."

Bayless also collected testimony from Rene Waller of Joplin, who also said that she had seen the Hornet Light before Route 66 was put in through Quapaw, Oklahoma. She stated that the original highway was a dirt road that was traveled infrequently. She had first seen the light in the late 1920s, when auto headlights would have been too seldom on the road to have created the effect of the spook light.

Mr. and Mrs. L. C. Ferguson of Joplin also stated that they had been familiar with the Hornet Light since 1910 and that when they first saw it, they were told that the light had been seen along the road for many years already.

These claims of the light's longevity were substantiated in the early 1960s by J. Leonard, a member of the Miami Indian tribe. He told Bayless that his parents had spoken of the light many times when he was a boy. He could personally remember seeing it for as long as he had been alive (he had been born in 1896) and according to stories at that time, the light had been in existence for several generations, or at least one hundred years. Another Native American from the area, Guy Jennison, recalled hearing about the light when he was a boy attending the Quapaw Mission School in 1892. By that time, it was a local topic of conversation, implying that reports of the light had been around for at least a few years. Jennison, like Leonard, believed that the light might have appeared several generations before, based on the Indian legends that had been suggested to explain its origin. Unfortunately, during the time of the Bayless investigation, there were few Native Americans left who had knowledge of when the stories originated.

Even without the earlier dates, Bayless was able to show that the Hornet Light existed prior to the use of automobiles in the area. He did not dispute the idea that some sightings could be caused by headlights, but he did debunk the idea that headlights could be the only cause. Others have suggested that perhaps lights from Quapaw or from mining camps in the area could have caused a refraction of light, thus creating the spook light, but there is little evidence to suggest this or to suggest that these stationary lights could manage to create a light that moved about and came and went as the Hornet Light does.

With that in mind, Raymond Bayless's investigations of the light should be considered groundbreaking. Although he certainly did not solve the mystery of the Hornet Light, he did manage to present some compelling evidence for its early existence. The only problem to come out of his investigations was that he managed, by showing how long the light had been around and by showing that not all of the sightings could be dismissed, to make the mystery even more perplexing.

Bayless was not the first, nor would he be the last, to investigate the Hornet Spook Light. Literally thousands of curiosity-seekers visit the Devil's Promenade each year, and many of those are serious researchers of the unknown. The old Spook Light Museum is gone now but long after Leslie Robertson came Garland "Spooky" Middleton, who also operated the place for a time. Along with displaying photographs and newspaper articles about the light, Middleton sold soda to tourists and entertained them with anecdotes about his own encounters with the mysterious light, like the time he saw it in a field near the museum. He said that the light appeared one night on the road, just after sunset, and began to roll like a ball, giving off sparks as it traveled along the gravel road. It entered a field where several cattle grazed and managed to move among the animals, not disturbing them at all.

On three different occasions, starting in the late 1990s, I visited Spook Light Road, each time hoping to get a glimpse of the elusive light. The first two times, I saw nothing, but I didn't give up hope that I might be at the right place at the right time at some point. Eventually, my persistence paid off. In December 2005, I returned to the site with a group of friends and, after a near case of frostbite, I finally got a look at this mysterious wonder. We had several false alarms during the night, with several of us thinking we saw the light, but each time it turned out to be headlights approaching along the lonely road. When the light did show up there was no mistaking it for anything else. One member of the group spotted it first and her response got the attention of several of the others who were standing together.

We saw the light appear at the crest of a small hill about fifty yards away, directly west of where we had parked along Spook Light Road. The light did not seem to have come up the hill, it just appeared there. Then it shot sideways to our right about seven or eight feet. The light was yellowish-orange in color and it left a faint "trail" behind it as it moved. The trail streaked out in a jagged motion, moving slightly up and down, and then blinked out into darkness. It was almost like a fireworks display on a summer night, shooting outward and then burning itself out as quickly as it had appeared. The sighting lasted no longer than ten seconds but it's not something that I will soon forget.

What is the Hornet Spook Light? No one knows, but I think that it's still described best in the words of the Army Corps of Engineers—a "mysterious light of unknown origin." Regardless of what it may be, one thing is certain: it's something that has to be seen, if possible. There are those who believe that the Hornet Light is slowly burning itself out, that sightings of the light are going to become more and more infrequent in the years to come. I hope that this is not the case, and not only for my own selfish desire to see the light again, but also for all of those who have not had the chance to experience this wonder themselves.

The Hornet Spook Light is one of America's greatest unsolved mysteries and since no one has managed to figure out the answers to this enigma yet, we need the spook light to be around for future generations to ponder for themselves.

Pythian Castle

Hidden away outside of Springfield are the looming battlements of what has come to be called Pythian Castle. Started in 1911 and requiring two years to build, the stone fortress was designed by a fraternal organization called the Knights of Pythias, who planned it as a home for the widows and orphans of its members.

As the years passed and the organization faded, the castle was taken over by the United States Army before finally being sold off as "surplus" and abandoned to time and the elements. Subsequent owners have managed to breathe life back into the place but have quickly found that not all of the building's past occupants have left. Stories abound of scores of lingering ghosts.

The Knights of Pythias was a fraternal order and secret society that was founded in Washington, D.C., in November 1864. It was the first fraternal organization to receive a charter under an act of the United States Congress. It was founded by Justin H. Rathbone, who had been inspired by a play by the Irish poet John Banim about Damon and Pythias, figures from Greek mythology who symbolized the trust and loyalty found in true friendship. Rathbone used the the legend as a basis for the order, building it around the ideals of loyalty, honor, and friendship.

The Pythian order grew rapidly in the late 1800s and at one time boasted over 700,000 members with more than 6,000 lodges across America. During the heyday of the order, twenty-two homes were constructed across the country to provide shelter for the widows and orphans of the lodge members. Eventually, as members grew older and interest in many fraternal organizations faded, the Knights of Pythias became smaller and began closing down the homes, which were expensive to operate. The order is still in existence today but membership is far less than what it was during the glory days of the society.

The Pythian Home near Springfield was much like the others built during this same time period. The 27,000-square-foot building, which was built to resemble a medieval castle, cost more than $150,000 to construct and was located on 53 acres outside of town. The foundation of the structure was made from Carthage stone, a strong variety of limestone that is quarried in the Ozarks. A steel framework was used to support the concrete floors, staircases, hallways, and ceilings. Pyrobar blocks (a gypsum-based material developed in the early 1900s that was used to prevent fires) made up all of the interior walls.

The castle was designed not only as a sort of glorified orphanage, but also as a place that would house and care for the widows of Knights of Pythias members. Because of this, it had an unusual design, which included a second-floor theater with 355 seats, a ticket booth, a projection room, and dressing rooms behind the stage. Funerals and church services were sometimes held there. The main floor had a foyer, meeting room, ballroom, dining room, and sitting parlors. The basement also had a gymnasium for the children; later, when the castle was used by the military, cells were installed there.

Behind the theater on the second floor were dormitories for the orphans and bedrooms for the widows. The orphans were segregated by sex, with boys on the right side of the building and girls on the left. There are many claims made that orphans at the Pythian Homes were not allowed to talk to one another or were abused in some way, but this is not the case. Most of those who grew up in Pythian Homes look back on the experience with happiness. The homes were well funded and the children well cared for. Most of the food served in the kitchen was grown on the property and the orphans were usually placed in charge of livestock-feeding and other chores in addition to their schoolwork. Being orphaned was undoubtedly a heartbreaking situation, but most residents look back with fondness to the days they spent at the Pythian Homes.

Around 1940, the U.S. Army's O'Reilly General Hospital Complex was erected next door to the Pythian Castle. Once completed, it contained over two hundred buildings on 160 acres of land and was used for the treatment of servicemen. The complex expanded after the start of World War II and in 1942, the military took over the Pythian Castle, purchasing it for $29,500. The castle was turned into the O'Reilly Service Club for enlisted men and began to be used for entertainment and the rehabilitation of soldiers wounded in battle.

The O'Reilly Service Club was said to be the best place of its kind in the country and featured Hollywood films in the theater, billiard rooms, a bowling alley, music-listening rooms, a library, sitting lounges, and more. Soldiers were able to attend USO dances and swing to sounds of entertainers like Cab Calloway, Benny Goodman, and Tommy Dorsey and laugh at the antics of performers like Bob Hope.

But not everything was happiness and light at the old castle. During this time, the castle was officially known as Building 501; the former laundry room behind it, listed as Building 503, was a military guardhouse. Located in the guardhouse and in the basement of the castle were cells that had been installed by the military to hold German prisoners of war. Little is known about the prisoners who were kept in those cells but it is said that they were used for labor duties throughout the complex. Rumors claim that some of these men were beaten and tortured and that at least one of them was killed in the steam tunnels under the castle, but whether or not these stories are true remains a mystery.

After the end of World War II, the castle became part of a Veterans Administration tuberculosis hospital, but this use only lasted for five years. In early 1952, the VA moved out and the property went on the market. In the interim, the Department of Defense allowed the Southwestern Power Administration, a federal agency, to temporarily use some of the buildings for storage. The castle itself was used by the Army Reserve. In 1955, the property was divided and sold; the National Guard obtained the property around the castle, the General Council of the Assemblies of God purchased much of the remaining property for the erection of the Evangel College of the Arts and Sciences, and several smaller groups bought various other sections of the grounds. In 1980, the Ozarks Area Community Action Corps leased the building and remained there until the end of 1993. In January 1994, the building was sold at auction to Gene and Rhonda Taylor, who owned it for the next six years. It was next purchased in 2000 by Linda and Frank Gray, who planned to use the building as a facility for the disabled, but their plans never materialized and the castle was sold again to its current owner, Tamara Finocchiao, who offers murder mystery weekends, rentals, and tours. She has worked hard to restore the building and meet the city's requirements, finally landing the castle in the National Register of Historic Places.

The old Pythian Castle has seen a lot of history pass through its doors over the last century and has seen many changes occur within its walls. But during all of this, time has, in many ways, stood still—at least when it comes to the resident ghosts.

The stories of ghosts at the castle began to emerge in the last few years, about the time that a greater number of people began visiting the place for mystery events and tours. While these stories may not date back many years, there are many of them; if you combine them all, then Pythian Castle is surely one of the most haunted locations in the state. Disembodied voices have frequently been heard within the walls, along with moaning and crying sounds that come from empty rooms and vacant corridors. Lights turn on and off by themselves and people frequently complain of batteries being drained in cameras and flashlights. Eerie cold spots come and go without warning, and objects and even heavy furniture move about on their own. The castle seems to play host to a number of ghosts, but who are they?

Some have suggested that the resident spirits are orphans who lived here back in the days when the Pythian Home was in operation. It does seem possible that some of the lonely little spirits who came to live in this new, strange place might have lingered behind, even though in the official records, only two children ever died here during the days of the orphanage. But perhaps the sounds of laughter, running feet, slamming doors, and mysterious voices are impressions left behind on the atmosphere of the castle, repeating themselves over time as a haunting. This could certainly explain some of the strange events that occur within the building's stone walls.

Could the ghosts be those of soldiers who stayed here during the time that it was a rehabilitation hospital? Or could they be simply servicemen who so enjoyed their time at the O'Reilly Service Club that they never wanted to leave? There have been encounters in the castle with men in uniform who often vanish when approached. The hard soles of shoes have been heard tapping on the stairs and down hallways, even when no one is there. Fire alarms sometimes go off, even though no one has pulled down the handle. Some claim to have been touched by unseen hands, usually experienced as a comforting pressure on the shoulder or back when no one is standing nearby.

And what of the German prisoners who were once housed in the basement? There are those who blame much of the haunting activity on these luckless men, doomed to remain in their cells even after death. Many people become unnerved, or even violently ill, when they go down into the lower levels of the basement. Doors have been heard to slam in that part of the building, even when it's empty, and others have heard chains drop and the sounds of a man loudly screaming. One night, according to the current owner, her dog stood at the top of the basement stairs and barked at something down in the darkness. She turned on the lights, but there was nothing there.

Whatever the identity of these ghosts might be, they seem satisfied with their residence at the Pythian Castle. Whether trapped there or lingering by choice, it seems as though they will be within the walls of the castle for many years to come.

Across the State

The Ghost of Stephens College

In 1862, the Civil War was raging in Missouri. It was a time of secessionists, Union loyalists, bloody battles, and deadly ambushes by guerilla fighters. The state of Missouri was soaked in blood. This war gave birth to one of the most enduring ghost stories of the region—the tale of Sarah June Wheeler.

The events began shortly after the March 1862 defeat of Sterling Price's forces at the Battle of Pea Ridge in Arkansas. This defeat brought an end to the organized Confederate resistance in Missouri, leaving only the bushwhackers and guerilla fighters to carry on, and paved the way for Union occupation of the state.

A short time after Pea Ridge, Federal forces under the command of Gen. Henry Halleck moved into Columbia, upsetting the populace and disturbing Dr. Hubert Williams, the president of the Columbia Baptist Female College (now Stephens College), and its dean, Miss Clara Armstrong. They feared for the safety of the young female students, as soldiers are not often known for their gentlemanly behavior. The finishing school for Southern ladies was located in the heart of the city and was at the time made up of one large structure that is now known as Senior Hall on the Stephens College campus.

One evening after dinner, a young seminary student named Sarah June Wheeler was hurrying up to her room. She had just stepped inside when a soldier climbed over her windowsill and staggered across the floor. Needless to say, Sarah was quite surprised, although even more shocked to see that the man wore not the uniform of the occupying Union soldiers, but the dirty and bedraggled gray of the Confederacy.

Before Sarah could call out for help, the young man had grabbed hold of her and clapped his hand over her mouth. She struggled to get free of him and the man suddenly just slumped to the floor, unconscious. Just then, the door to the room opened and Sarah's roommate, Margaret Baker, came inside. She was also surprised to see a Confederate soldier, although not as frightened as Sarah had been. Margaret had been born and raised in Arkansas and was fiercely loyal to the Confederacy. Instead of payment to the school, her father had sent two slaves who cooked, cleaned, and worked in the school's laundry.

The young soldier had been injured and was bleeding. The girls tended to his wounds and when he work up, he told them that he had not eaten in days. They helped him into a chair and then Margaret sent her servants to bring back a tray of food from the kitchen. They were given strict instructions to say nothing of the soldier.

The man introduced himself as Corporal Isaac Johnson from Mississippi. He said that he had fought at Pea Ridge and had recently escaped from a prison in Illinois, traveling by night and hiding during the day. His father had been killed in the earlier fighting and Johnson had vowed to avenge his death in some way. The plan that he had come up with was to sneak into Columbia and assassinate General Halleck.

There was something about the young man that appealed to the girls, especially to Sarah, and they agreed to try and keep him safe. Sarah hid Johnson away, brought him food, and talked with into the early hours of the morning. It was not long before the young couple had fallen in love. But their relationship was doomed from the start.

Someone, possibly one of Margaret's slaves, let the secret slip that a Confederate soldier was hiding at the school. Eventually, word reached General Halleck's staff. Union troopers followed a

trail of blood to the school, but they wouldn't enter the grounds. They were under orders from General Halleck not to trespass on the grounds of the girls' school; doing so was considered improper. Only officers later entered the school when they had proof the soldier was hiding there. The young ladies, mostly Southerners, stood by the iron fence and taunted them but there was nothing they could do. Finally, General Halleck paid a call on Dr. Williams and warned him that the school would be closed unless the soldier was captured.

That evening, Dr. Williams addressed the young women and explained to them what Halleck had threatened. Quickly, Sarah returned to her room and urged Johnson to surrender, but he had a better idea. He had stolen a suit from Dr. Williams' closet; in this disguise, he would escape to Canada.

The plan seemed perfect, but Sarah's secret had somehow become common knowledge among the other young women at the school. A crowd gathered near Sarah's room and urged her to turn the soldier over the Federals. The clamor grew louder until Dr. Williams learned what was going on. Accompanied by General Halleck, he arrived at Sarah's room. Halleck announced that the school was now closed and all of the girls were told to pack their belongings before first light.

Just then, Corporal Johnson appeared from Sarah's room and surrendered himself. He begged that Halleck let the students remain and explained that he had been hiding there without their knowledge. Halleck reluctantly agreed and proceeded to arrest Johnson as a spy. Ironically, as he was now wearing civilian clothing, he was no longer afforded the rights of a soldier. A spy who was captured behind enemy lines was sentenced to death.

Three nights later, Corporal Isaac Johnson was executed in the street near the school. Soon after the last shots rang out, the body of Sarah June Wheeler was discovered outside of the school. She had thrown herself from an upper window, taking her own life in hopes of joining her lover in death.

In another version of the story, Sarah hanged herself from the bell tower of the school; in later years, Stephens College students often visited the tower to hold séances, hoping to communicate with Sarah's ghost. They probably had little luck, since the school did not actually have a bell tower in 1862. It was not constructed until the 1870s. Another story claims that Sarah and Isaac actually escaped from the school but died as they tried to cross the flooded waters of Hinkson Creek.

Regardless of how she actually died, it is believed that Sarah still walks at her former school, which is now Senior Hall. It has been restored today to look much like it did when she lived there and legend has it that she is searching for the ghost of Corporal Johnson, hoping to be reunited with him in the afterlife.

There are many who dismiss the stories of Sarah and her unlucky soldier as nothing more than folklore, but others claim that unusual things happen in Senior Hall. On Halloween 1971, a reporter named Bob M. Gassaway who worked for a local newspaper spent the night in the building with some of the students and instructors who wanted to have a séance and try to contact Sarah. They climbed into the tower and placed their candles on the floor. At that moment, the door slammed, the candles went out, and one of the girls in the group screamed and passed out. There was a commotion in the hallway. It was the reporter trying to get into the room. He demanded to know if anyone else had seen what he had seen—a man in a uniform and a woman in a long dress!

On November 1, 1971, Gassaway wrote, "There was the sound of slow steps at first. When they stopped, deep breathing became audible. I waited for the person to come through the door. And waited. And waited. Finally I took the initiative, hauled myself from the floor and moved to the hallway's mouth. Halfway down the hall . . . I see the figure of a man. Then the swish of a woman's long skirt caught my eye as the man dropped into a half crouch, his left hand outstretched as if to ward something off. Then both figures disappeared down the stairs—quietly."

Senior Hall was renovated and remodeled in the 1990s and is now home to music and dance classes, and yet the ghost stories persist.

The James Family Farm

Jesse James always maintained that he only became an outlaw because the "government pushed him to it." A product of the Civil War era, he is remembered today as Missouri's greatest outlaw. In his time, he was glorified as a misunderstood, good man who had gone bad due to the carpetbaggers, the greedy bankers, and the powerful railroads. He has been called "America's Robin Hood," but he and his brother and their fellow gang members did not steal from the rich and give to the poor—they stole from everyone, kept the loot for themselves, and killed a lot of people along the way.

It should come as no surprise that there are hauntings connected with the life and crimes of Jesse James, although strangely, those hauntings seem to be most connected with the violent deeds that were carried out against the James family, rather than with anything Jesse did during his lifetime.

The James family farm near Kearney, Missouri, is believed to be haunted. It was here that Jesse's mother, Zerelda Cole James Sims Samuel, married three different husbands and bore eight children. It was also here that she saw her son Archie murdered by Pinkerton detectives in an attack where she lost her own right hand. She also saw one of her husbands tortured and driven insane on this land and she lived in this house while her two famous outlaw sons eluded capture, sometimes with her devoted assistance. She also guarded the property where her son Jesse, after his murder, was buried in a grave that she could see from her bedroom window. Zerelda spent her years of widowhood on the farm, as did her daughter-in-law, Annie Ralston James.

And mostly, they remained here alone save for the company of their household servants, a family of slaves who remained at the farm long after they were set free.

Were the stories of hauntings on the farm created by years of loneliness and isolation, overactive imaginations that saw lights in the trees and heard voices where none should be heard? Or were other dark events at work here, generating the hauntings from the history of this place?

The outlaw career of Jesse James was born of the Civil War conflicts that occurred in the state of Missouri. It was a state torn in two directions. The state's early settlers had come from the South, yet Missouri's economy was linked directly to that of the North. The state's elected officials were mainly secessionists and intended to link Missouri, which had entered the Union as a slave state, to the Confederacy. A number of battles were fought in the state; in fact, a total of 1,162 battles and skirmishes were fought in Missouri during the official years of the war, a total exceeded only by Virginia and Tennessee.

More dangerous than the regular army campaigns were the bushwhacking raids carried out by the guerilla fighters. The leading bands, under William Clarke Quantrill, "Bloody Bill" Anderson, George Todd, and William Gregg, were mostly made up of backwoods farm boys. All of them seemed to share one thing: they all came from families who had been harassed, intimidated, robbed, burned out, or murdered by Federal soldiers.

These men became the forerunners of the outlaws who would later wreak havoc in the West. They only used light weapons, but they attacked with an element of surprise that only small bands of riders can utilize. They were not above sneak attacks, guerilla warfare, or shooting their enemies in the back. Thanks to the amount of local support they enjoyed, they found it easy to outmatch detachments of Union troops. Often, they would even dress in blue uniforms and hail the Federal columns as comrades before opening fire on them. It was a brutal and ruthless method of fighting, but lethally effective. The bushwhacking gangs served as a training ground for men like Jesse James.

Jesse James came from humble roots along the western edge of Missouri. His father, Robert Sallee James, was a farmer and Baptist preacher who graduated from Georgetown College in Kentucky in 1843. Two years later, he met Zerelda Cole at a revival meeting and married her. The couple moved from Kentucky to Missouri, where Robert became the pastor of a small Baptist church outside of Kearney. They settled on a farm in Clay County, where Zerelda gave birth to four children named Alexander Franklin (Frank), Robert (who only lived thirty-three days), Jesse Woodson, and Susan Lavina.

Reverend James was a well-liked and respected man in the community and in 1850, he was asked to serve as chaplain to a wagon train of local men who were going west to California to search for gold. Little is known of this adventure, save for the fact that Reverend James died in a Placerville mining camp on August 18, 1850, and was buried in an unmarked grave.

Zerelda, faced with raising her children alone, married a neighboring farmer in 1852. He was killed in a horse accident a short time later, and in 1855, she married Dr. Rueben Samuel, a kindly physician and farmer. She would go on to raise four more children with Dr. Samuel, who became the only father the James children would ever know. A later child, Archie, was born mildly retarded and he was kept close to home. His older brothers doted on the boy and Archie's tragic death in 1875 would add fuel to Jesse's hatred of the authorities.

The James brothers stayed on the farm started by their father, and thanks to Dr. Samuel's purchase of adjoining property, the James holdings grew. Frank and Jesse farmed through their teenage years, but in time the violence of the outside world began to intrude on their peaceful farm life. The area where the James family lived was near the turbulent Missouri-Kansas border. Zerelda, a formidable frontier woman, had been raised in Kentucky and was a slave owner, so there was no question that her sympathies were directed toward the South. In May 1861, Frank James enlisted in the Confederate Army. He fought under Gen. Sterling Price in the Battle of Wilson's Creek in southwest Missouri, then, after a brief period at home, joined up with Quantrill and his band of raiders. Frank and his friend Thomas Coleman "Cole" Younger, from Lee's Summit, Missouri, were with Quantrill during a 1863 raid on Lawrence, Kansas, that left nearly two hundred men dead.

The Lawrence Massacre remains one of the bloodiest events in the history of Kansas and the pro-Union Jayhawkers wasted no time in retaliating. A day after the attack, surviving citizens of Lawrence lynched a member of Quantrill's raiders caught in town. On August 25, Gen. Thomas Ewing authorized orders that evicted thousands of Missourians in four counties from their homes near the Kansas border. Virtually everything in these counties was burned to the ground. The raids were vicious, thorough, and indiscriminate and left the western part of the state wasted and in flames.

The retaliation continued for months afterward. Just three months after the Lawrence raid, a party of Union soldiers invaded the Samuel–James family farm, looking for information about the location of Quantrill's camp. Jesse, who was just fifteen years old at the time, was questioned, then horse-whipped when he refused to answer the soldiers' questions. Dr. Samuel, who also denied knowing where the raider's camp was located, was dragged from his house and was repeatedly hanged from a tree in the yard. Somehow, the doctor managed to survive the interrogation, but his mental state was so affected by the ordeal that he was placed in an asylum in St. Joseph afterward. He remained there until his death in 1908.

Jesse, now with a burning hatred for the Union, joined up with the guerillas in 1864. He went to war under the command of Bloody Bill Anderson, who had taken over most of the resistance following Quantrill's retreat to Texas after the Lawrence raid. Jesse was by then an expert horseman and a crack shot with his pistols.

Jesse and Frank James rose to such prominence during the war that the Samuels were singled out for persecution by Union troops, who raided the farm and forced the family to move to Nebraska. After the war, Frank and Jesse returned to the vacant farm. As guerilla fighters that were not part of the regular Confederate army, they were considered outlaws. Later in 1865, when a general amnesty was offered to guerillas, Jesse led a small band toward Lexington intending to surrender. A company of Union soldiers, ignoring the amnesty, hid in an ambush and opened fire on the guerillas. Jesse was shot from his horse, a bullet puncturing his lung, but he managed to crawl into the underbrush. He was later found by a friendly farmer, who bandaged his wounds and helped him get to his mother's home.

During his convalescence, Jesse met his cousin, Zerelda Mimms, who had been named after his mother. She nursed him back to health and the two fell in love. Zee, as she was called, was too young to marry but they made plans for the future. Nine years later, they took their wedding vows. Jesse remained fiercely devoted to her all his life.

Jesse eventually returned home to Kearney, where he and Frank worked the farm. They lived in a constant state of alert. Frank and Jesse always wore guns, even to church, and usually kept a horse saddled in the barn in case Union soldiers came to the farm. They were still technically outlaws since they had never officially surrendered after the war came to an end. They soon decided to put that "outlaw" moniker to the test.

The first bank robbery attributed to the James brothers occurred on February 13, 1866. They carried off $60,000, almost without incident, from the Clay County Savings Bank in Liberty, Missouri. It was the first daylight bank robbery in American history—and the birth of a legend.

In the years that followed, the James Gang, which was usually made up of Jesse and Frank and Cole, Jim, and Bon Younger, with others occasionally along for the ride, became one of the most famous outlaw gangs in American history. They became the first real bank robbers that the country had ever seen and operated with almost full impunity thanks to their friends and neighbors in the region. Much of this was due to the public relations campaign started by their mother, Zerelda, during which the brothers claimed innocence for their crimes. If they had done anything wrong, it was because they were driven to it by Yankee bankers and railroad magnates, who had imposed impossible farm mortgages on the common man so that they could foreclose on their property using underhanded land-grabbing schemes. To some degree, this was true, but it ignored the murders that had been carried out in the course of the rebellion against the banks. If the publicity campaign did anything, though, it created the folktales of the James gang as Robin Hood figures, stealing from the rich and giving to the poor. It created a fierce loyalty for the boys that would last until the end of the James brothers' infamous careers. Over the course of the next sixteen years, the James-Younger Gang would achieve both fame and notoriety.

After a string of daring robberies, Jesse finally decided to marry Zee Simms, who had insisted that if he did not marry her, she would not see him anymore. Jesse had been courting her for years, meeting in backwoods cabins and wilderness retreats. Jesse and Zee went to Kansas City and got married, and then traveled to Galveston, Texas, on a honeymoon. Afterward, they returned to Kearney and settled into a home of their own. Jesse had no intention of ending his life of crime but it is believed that Zee looked the other way out of love. Jesse was desperately in love with his wife and was a devoted husband and father. The couple produced two children, Jesse Junior and Mary. Frank also married around this time, eloping with Annie Ralston, a union that would produce a son, Robert, in 1878.

While Jesse and Frank were settling into their married lives, the Pinkerton Detective Agency was increasing its efforts to try and hunt them down. The agency had first been hired in 1871 by several banks and railroads to try and collar the James gang.

On January 26, 1875, the Pinkertons attacked the James family farm, believing that Frank and Jesse were there. A force of Pinkerton detectives, brought in by special train, surrounded the house and demanded that Frank and Jesse come outside. A light went out in an upper window so one of the Pinkertons tossed an incendiary device of some sort through the window. It exploded with a deafening roar. The resulting explosion tore through Archie Samuel and mangled Zerelda's right arm so badly that it had to be amputated at the elbow. Archie died within the hour, writing in agony. Jesse and Frank had been nowhere near the farm.

No other act could have earned more sympathy for the James brothers. The newspapers called it an "inexcusable and cowardly deed," crucifying the Pinkertons and labeling them as child-killers and monsters who attacked defenseless women. Allan Pinkerton defended the actions of his agents, claiming the device that was thrown through the window was simply a flare. It is believed that it was actually a grenade-type explosive that had been obtained at the federal arsenal in Rock Island, Illinois. Jesse was so enraged over Archie's murder that he spent long hours planning Pinkerton's assassination. He even took a train to Chicago and spent hours waiting at the Pinkerton headquarters, planning to shoot the man on sight. He later told a friend that he saw Pinkerton but did not shoot him on the crowded Chicago street. He wanted to give him a fair chance, he said.

The Jameses and Youngers continued to commit robberies, only faltering after a disastrous raid in Northfield, Minnesota, caused the deaths of the several gang members and the capture of others. Frank and Jesse managed to escape into the Dakota Territory in the aftermath and disappeared for a time. The Northfield raid made national headlines and Jesse and Frank James became the most wanted men in America—but they were nowhere to be found. Lawmen and bounty hunters scoured Minnesota, Wisconsin, and Iowa as the brothers moved slowly south and west. They traveled on foot for a while, and then stole fresh horses, which they later abandoned. They slept in empty houses and barns during the day and only traveled at night. It took them nearly three weeks to make it home but when they arrived, they realized that they were too notorious to remain on their Missouri farms. The Northfield raid marked the beginning of the end for the James brothers.

The James brothers disappeared for a time but soon ran out of money, so they organized a new gang in the fall of 1879. After several robberies, they went quiet for a time and then returned to Missouri in July 1881. On July 15, they stopped a Chicago, Rock Island & Pacific train at Winston and when a passenger tried to interfere with the robbery, Jesse shot him dead. The train engineer refused to follow Jesse's orders and was also gunned down. The outlaws only got $600 from this bloody robbery, but it prompted Missouri governor Thomas Crittenden to offer a $10,000 reward for the arrest and conviction of Jesse and Frank James.

This amount of money was an astronomical sum in those days, but in earlier times, it would not have caused thoughts of betrayal among members of the James gang. The Younger brothers were blood kin to the James brothers and absolutely loyal. Other earlier gang members were fellow veterans of the guerilla bands of the Civil War and were tied to Jesse and Frank through old connections and military loyalties. But the new members that Jesse had recruited to the gang had little or no allegiance to them. This included Robert and Charles Ford, two young men who learned of the reward and planned to murder Jesse. After making arrangements to collect the reward from Governor Crittenden, Robert Ford went to St. Joseph to meet with Jesse.

Jesse was living in St. Joseph under the name Robert Howard and on April 3, 1882, he called the Fords to his home to discuss the robbery of the Platte County Bank. Jesse was relaxing in the parlor, reading the newspaper, and Zee was working in the kitchen. The three men sat down and talked for a while and then Charles went out into the backyard while Robert made small talk with Jesse. As he was reading, Jesse glanced up and noticed that a framed needlepoint picture, done by his mother, was hanging crookedly on the wall. He moved a cane chair over to the wall and stepped up to straighten it, his back to the room. This was the opportunity Robert Ford had been waiting for. He pulled out a revolver and shot Jesse just below the right ear, killing him.

The news of Jesse's death made headlines in almost every newspaper in the country. The newspapers and dime novelists who had churned out endless stories about the outlaw for years mourned his passing. Almost immediately, the legend and lore of Jesse James began to be embellished to make it seem that he had lived and died as a hero, not a murderous outlaw. The legend still continues to this day.

After an inquest, Jesse's body was packed in ice and taken by train to Kearney, where he was displayed and viewed by hundreds of friends and admirers. Jesse was later buried on the family farm with only close family and friends present. His seven-foot-deep grave was placed near Zerelda's front door so that she could keep an eye out for trespassers and souvenir hunters. Later, when Zerelda could no longer live alone, her son's body was moved to the Mount Olivet Cemetery in town. Zee died in 1900 and was buried next to her husband.

Hauntings at the James family farm have been reported for many years but it seems likely the strange events have little to do with the violence carried out by Jesse James and more to do with the Pinkertons' violent raid on the farm in 1875, the raid that left Zerelda Samuel badly injured and Archie dead.

Over the years, staff members and volunteers at the museum that now occupies the property have had weird experiences inside the old farmhouse where the violence occurred. Doors have slammed closed on their own, lights have been seen moving about in the locked house, and a presence has been so intense in the house that one guide refused to remain there alone.

Another staff member admitted that she had, on more than one occasion, heard the voices of men in the woods near the house and heard the sounds of restless horses when no horses were present. Once, she was so sure that the sounds were real that she went out into the woods to search for the horses. However, she found no tracks or signs that any horses had been there.

The strange sounds, opening and closing doors, and mysterious lights continue to be experienced on the James family farm. Are they signs that restless ghosts are nearby, or are the eerie happenings merely memories from the past, stuck like a needle on an old Victrola, playing over and over again through the years?

The Elms

Located in the starkly silent town of Excelsior Springs is the Elms Resort Hotel and Spa. It is a place, like the town that surrounds it, that time has forgotten. Walking into the hotel today is like stepping back into 1912, when the spa was in its heyday and people were coming from all over the state to take in the healing waters of the area's mineral springs. During its glory years in the early twentieth century, the Elms hosted gangsters, professional athletes, celebrities, and at least two American presidents. To this day, it continues to play host to guests who checked in, but have never checked out.

In the summer of 1880, Indians and hunters told a western Missouri settler named Travis Mellion about some natural springs in the area that had curative powers. Mellion had a daughter who was plagued by consumption (tuberculosis) and he decided to see if the waters helped her. Just weeks after bathing in the spring and drinking the water, she was reportedly cured. Another man, Frederick Kigler, tried the waters for a leg problem and apparently achieved the same results. In a short time, the stories of the springs spread and people began traveling great distances to look for their own cures. Within a year, more than two hundred homes had been built in the area and the town of Excelsior Springs was born.

In 1888, the Excelsior Springs Company built the first Elms Hotel amidst the rolling lands and lush trees on the edge of town. The three-story hotel hosted scores of visitors every season, and offered large, shaded verandas on all four sides, a live orchestra, a large heated swimming pool, a bowling alley, a billiards room, and a target range for skeet shooting.

Unfortunately, in 1898, the beautiful hotel was destroyed in a fire. Although no one was injured, the structure was a total loss. Plans were made to rebuild the place but due to various delays, construction did not begin on the new Elms until 1908. In July 1909, the new Elms had its second grand opening and the popularity of the place continued to spread—but only for two short years. On October 29, 1910, the hotel burned down again. Following a large party in the Grand Ballroom, a boiler ignited and the fire spread throughout the interior and set the roof ablaze. The hotel was lost once again, but thankfully, no one was killed—no

guests, anyway. Rumor has it that some staff members who were working on the boiler in the basement died in the blaze. Their ghosts are still said to be haunting the hotel, banging on the pipes in the walls. Those who have dismissed such stories as nothing more than pipes that make noise when the heat turns on have to be told that those pipes are no longer connected to the heating system.

The owners were again determined to rebuild after the 1910 fire. In order to do this, they had to sell off some of the property surrounding the hotel to raise the funds. Work began on the new structure soon after, this time with efforts to make the hotel as fireproof as possible. Missouri limestone was used for the principal work, along with steel frames and reinforced concrete. The hotel had its final grand opening on September 7, 1912, drawing a crowd of more than three thousand people.

Business at the hotel boomed during the Prohibition era, and it became a very popular speakeasy, serving alcohol during a time when it was illegal across the country. The Elms attracted all sorts of guests during this time, from average folks to the cream of Kansas City society. It also played host to a number of gangsters, including Chicago mobster Al Capone, who was known to conduct all-night drinking and gambling parties in his suite of rooms. Whenever he stayed at the Elms, Capone would line up all of the staff members before he left and tip each of them with a $100 bill. Needless to say, he was one of the more popular guests of the 1920s.

One of the guests from this era has never checked out of the hotel. He was killed during the violent Prohibition days and now reportedly haunts the European lap pool. Gangsters often stored their booze and held parties in a blocked-off section of the hotel and this unlucky spirit was a man who crossed the wrong bootlegger and got a bullet for his trouble.

During the Depression, the hotel fell on hard times and closed down for a while. In the late 1930s, though, it opened again and it thrived during World War II, again hosting both famous guests and ordinary people who came to take in the legendary waters. During the 1948 presidential election, Harry S. Truman sought refuge at the hotel when it appeared that he was losing his reelection bid. However, in the wee hours of the morning, he was awakened by his aides informing him that he had, in fact, won the election. A short time later, he was photographed holding the now-famous copy of the *Chicago Tribune* that mistakenly declared Thomas Dewey the winner.

The late 1960s dealt a serious blow to the Elms when the U.S. government ruled that mineral water treatments could no longer be covered by insurance. People largely stopped coming to town and most of the local water sources were capped. Other hotels in town were closed, boarded up, and abandoned—but not the Elms. While much of Excelsior Springs was closed down, the old hotel has managed to endure, fully restored to its former glory and still hosting hundreds of guests every year.

The Elms, like many historic hotels, seems to be filled with unearthly guests. Both guests and staff report the feeling of mysterious presences throughout the building. A chandelier has been reported shaking in the Grand Ballroom and once, a manager chased the sound of a phantom vacuum cleaner as it traveled about one floor of the hotel. Could it have been in the ghostly hands of the maid who has been seen wearing a 1920s-style uniform? She has been seen many times by guests and employees. Staffers feel that she is only there to watch today's housekeeping staff to ensure that they are doing their work correctly.

Another resident ghost seems to be that of a former guest. The spectral woman walks through the hotel looking for her child. Distressed, she has been known to pull people's hair or throw things across the room in despair.

There are two allegedly haunted rooms at the Elms, Room 505 and Room 501. The presence in Room 505 is said to have once bumped a staff member and then locked him inside of the room. According to reports, the employee eventually managed to get out of the room but refused to ever go back into it again.

Early one morning, around 2:00 A.M., the hotel's fire alarm went off. While everyone was waiting for the fire department to arrive, a phone at the front desk began ringing. There was no one on the other end of the line. It rang again and once more, there was no one there. The call was coming from Room 501. One of the front desk managers went up to the room, but it was empty. Thinking that perhaps there was something wrong with the line, he unplugged the phone from the wall and went back downstairs.

Before he made it to the desk, staff members reported that it had rung again—after the manager had unplugged it.

Who haunts the Elms? Staff members from the past, former guests, or both? While the ghosts' identities may remain a mystery, it's no surprise that they chose to stay behind at this fascinating and atmospheric spot, where the past is never far away from the present.

Kansas City's Union Station

The sun was shining brightly over Kansas City, Missouri, on the morning of June 17, 1933. Outside Union Station, there was the usual flurry of activity as people came and went on the trains and crowds milled about, hurrying to catch a train as it was leaving the station or greeting loved ones who had just arrived by rail.

Suddenly, the pleasant day was shattered by the sound of machine-gun fire echoing from the plaza parking lot. People began to scream and run for their lives, automobile tires squealed, men's voices cried out in anger, and over and over came the harsh retorts of gunfire. By the time it finally came to an end, five men were dead and two others were wounded. Blood-soaked bodies were twisted inside a bullet-scarred 1932 Chevrolet and others lay sprawled on the pavement outside.

What no one knew in those panicked moments was that six of the victims were law-enforcement officers, three of whom were agents of the Justice Department's Bureau of Investigation. The seventh man, who lay dead with most of his head blown away, was a criminal who the cops and feds were returning to Leavenworth, a prison from which he had made one of his famous escapes. His name was Frank Nash and he was one of the most successful bank robbers of the Depression era. Nash had been nicknamed "Jelly" because of his uncanny ability to escape from even the most secure prisons.

But it was not only prison that Frank Nash escaped from. Some say that on the day of the "Kansas City Massacre," Nash managed to escape from the grave as well. His body may have been shattered by bullets that morning, but his spirit managed to survive.

Frank Nash never achieved the notoriety that was given to the famous bank robbers of the 1930s, but he enjoyed a career that was just as profitable and perhaps even more daring than most. His life of crime began with a steady stream of burglaries but turned to murder when he came to believe one of his accomplices was talking to the police. Nash was arrested and brought to trial but managed to get acquitted. He then murdered a witness who had testified against him and, for that, he was sentenced to serve a life term at Oklahoma's McAlester State Prison. Nash was a model prisoner, and in July 1918 he was given a full pardon and released. In a short time, he was back to committing crimes again. In and out of prison for the next few years, he was arrested in 1923 for U.S. mail robbery that got him sentenced to the federal prison at Leavenworth. He again behaved well at Leavenworth and was made a trusty. After being given an outside assignment in October 1930, he calmly walked away from the prison and disappeared.

What Nash did after his escape is not known for sure. He hooked up with the infamous Barker-Karpis gang for some time. Nash is also believed to have worked briefly for the Capone mob, with the rackets in Kansas City, and with several small outfits, organizing and carrying out robberies and burglaries.

It wasn't long before Nash was arrested again, this time in the well-known underworld hangout of Hot Springs, Arkansas. On June 16, 1933, Agents Frank C. Smith and F. Joseph Lackey from the Bureau of Investigation's Oklahoma City office spotted Nash lounging with a bottle of beer in front of the cigar store. They followed him to a horse-betting parlor, where he was placed under arrest.

The two Bureau of Investigation agents drove into Fort Smith. At 8:30 P.M., they took their manacled prisoner aboard the Missouri Pacific Flyer headed for Kansas City. They would be met there the following morning by more federal officers and local police officers, who would accompany them on the final leg of their trip to Leavenworth. Realizing that Nash's criminal friends might try to help him escape, the agents kept their route a secret.

Word about Nash's capture spread, eventually reaching Verne Miller, a member of the Barker-Karpis gang who was living in Kansas City. He was an expert marksman who had learned his craft as a machine-gunner during World War I. After being discharged from the Army, he returned home to South Dakota where his prowess with firearms earned him a job as a policeman. He was later elected sheriff but Miller felt constricted by the law and turned to a life of crime, first as a bootlegger and later as a bank robber. After a series of arrests, he ended up in St. Paul, Minnesota, where he met Barker and Karpis, and then drifted to Chicago, where he was hired out as a gunman.

Miller learned that an unnamed prisoner was heading to Kansas City by train and he began making arrangements to meet him. On the morning of June 17, there were a number of people waiting to see "Jelly" Nash. Federal agents Raymond Caffrey and R. E. Vetterli and city detectives W. J. "Red" Grooms and Frank Hermanson were waiting to escort Nash to Leavenworth in their car. Also waiting were five or more gangsters, the would-be rescuers of Frank Nash. One of them was definitely Verne Miller but the identities of the others are unkown to this day.

When the Missouri Pacific Flyer pulled into the station, Agent Lackey instructed Smith to stay with Nash in the stateroom while he went to the loading platform to find his contacts. Establishing their credentials to be legitimate, Lackey then asked the men to help him survey the immediate area. All were satisfied that nothing appeared out of the ordinary. Lackey then went back to the train to retrieve Nash. As Miller and the other waiting gangsters surveyed the scene and determined that the prisoner was Nash, they went out to the parking lot and took up positions among the parked automobiles.

Nash was led from the train platform and through the station toward the outdoor plaza by the two agents, Lackey and Smith, who both carried shotguns, and by Otto Reed, police chief of McAlester, Oklahoma. The trio, joined by the local lawmen, began to get into a Chevrolet that was parked in the plaza. Nash got into the front seat and Lackey, Smith, and Reed got into the back. Agent Caffrey walked around the automobile to the driver's side when a thunderous voice yelled at the lawmen from across the parking lot, "Up, up! Get 'em up!"

Frozen in shock, the agents and the detectives looked up to see three men standing on the running boards of a nearby car, pointing machine guns in their direction. The man who had yelled at them waved his weapon back and forth while another, heavy-set man pointed the muzzle of his gun directly at their windshield. For the next several moments, the entire parking lot was frozen in time. The lawmen dared not move and bystanders stood gaping at the drama that was playing out in front of them. Police detective Red Grooms moved first. He jerked his pistol out and squeezed off two shots, hitting the heavyset man in the arm.

The wounded gangster never paused. He shouted, "Let 'em have it!" A second later, he pulled the trigger of his machine gun and he and the others raked the Chevrolet with bullets. Burning lead ripped into the metal body of the car and shattered the window glass. Agent Caffrey spun to the pavement, dead before he hit the ground. Police Chief Reed took several bullets to the chest and fell to the floor of the car. Agents Smith and Lackey were also hit several times and pitched forward onto the floorboards. Lackey somehow managed to pull himself up and thrust his revolver out the window, returning a few shots. The weapon was shot out of his hand. Agent Vetterli and detectives Grooms and Hermanson were all wounded and fell to the pavement, scrambling for any cover they could find.

Inside the car, Nash waved frantically at the gangsters with handcuffed wrists. He screamed at them, "For God's sake, don't shoot me!" His voice was silenced by machine-gun fire as bullets ripped away most of his head.

Bystanders ran screaming for cover as bullets cut through the air. Many ducked behind cars, while others merely dropped to the pavement and covered their heads with their hands. Lottie West, a caseworker for the Traveler's Aid Society, witnessed the massacre from the station. She spotted a police officer that she knew, Mike Fanning, who came running to see what was going on in the parking lot. She screamed at him, "They're killing everybody!"

Bullets were now bouncing into the pavement in front of the car. They tore into the already-wounded lawmen, killing detectives Grooms and Hermanson. The big man with the machine gun fired another volley into the car, and then jumped into a light-colored Oldsmobile, which roared west towards Broadway.

The lawmen's Chevrolet was in shambles. In the front seat, a man was dead under the steering wheel. On the rear seat was another dead man; on the right was an unconscious man. A fourth man lay facedown on the floor. A pool of blood began to gather on the pavement. Five men were dead: federal agent Caffrey, Chief

Reed, detectives Hermanson and Grooms, and Frank Nash, the man the shooting supposedly had been designed to set free.

In hours, newspapers across the country screamed headlines about the "Kansas City Massacre." The public was shocked and federal agents and local lawmen scoured the Kansas and Missouri countryside looking for the escaped gunmen. Witnesses tentatively identified one of the killers as Verne Miller. Miller was known for his violent temper and often erratic behavior and the Kansas City Massacre had all of the earmarks of the kind of unstable operation that he would plan. In the hours after the massacre, the police went to Miller's home but found that he had fled. They found bloody rags in his living room, but nothing else. Miller and his current girlfriend, Vivian Mathias, had escaped to Chicago. On October 31, 1933, federal agents raided their apartment but again, Miller had escaped. Mathias was taken into custody and charged with harboring a fugitive.

Almost a month later, on November 29, Miller's naked and mutilated corpse was found in a roadside ditch outside Detroit. His hands and feet were tied and he appeared to have been tortured before his death. His skin had been burned with flatirons, an ice pick had been used on his tongue and face, and he had been badly beaten. His captors had finished him off by crushing his skull with some sort of heavy object. To the investigators who had been pursuing him, Miller's murder had all of the signs of an organized crime execution. But what happened?

One of the most prevalent theories behind the Kansas City Massacre is that it was never designed to help Frank Nash escape from custody, but rather to make sure that he was permanently silenced. Many believe that powerful figures in the underworld were afraid that Nash might talk about things he knew to stay out of prison, endangering their operations. Rather than let him be taken into custody, they had him killed—and hired Miller to pull the trigger. Then, because he knew who had ordered the hit to be carried out, he was killed as well.

Another rumor, which circulated in mob circles, suggests that the mobsters may not have been the ones who really killed Frank Nash. He may have accidentally been killed by a federal agent instead. There was (and still is) speculation that the wounds that killed Frank Nash and Agent Caffrey, both in the front seat of the car, may have been caused by a weapon that was in the backseat, in the hands of another federal agent. The story has persisted that when the fighting broke out, the agent began fumbling with the action of an unfamiliar 16-gauge shotgun that was loaded with steel ball bearings instead of the customary lead buckshot. The shotgun then went off by accident, blowing most of Nash's head all over the roof of the car and fatally wounding Agent Caffrey. Some of the ball bearings were reportedly found in the agent's body during an autopsy.

Whatever happened, the end result was the same: Frank "Jelly" Nash had his life instantly snuffed out. Whether he was killed by accident by a shot that he never saw coming, or whether he was slain by his friend Verne Miller, his spirit now refuses to rest. To this day, local stories have it, his ghost can still be found wandering through Union Station. Does he repeat that last walk through the station on his way to the lawmen's car—and to his doom? Or is he searching for his killers, wondering what became of the men who betrayed him back in 1933?

Stories of a haunting have swirled about Union Station for many years. Some people have reported seeing figures of men in dark suits outside the building, near where the massacre took place. When approached, these figures always vanish. There are also stories of footsteps being heard on the pavement outside, and inside the building in the corridor leading out to the parking lot. Some have surmised that these phantom footsteps may be a reenactment of the last steps taken by Frank Nash and the federal agents as they walked to their doom.

The ghost of Frank Nash is perhaps the most commonly reported specter connected to the massacre. One of the most compelling stories about Nash's spirit at Union Station came from a former night security guard. According to the guard, she was working security dispatch with her supervisor when the two of them looked at one of the many security surveillance camera screens and saw a man sitting on a bench overlooking the station's Grand Hall. Another guard was dispatched to find out who this man was, and why he was still in the building after hours. As the guard and her supervisor looked closer at the security screen, though, they realized that the figure they were observing seemed to have no head! As they continued to watch the screen, they saw the guard who had been sent to the area also appear on the screen. He stopped walking just a few yards away from where the mysterious figure was sitting and looked around. A few moments later, the radio crackled to life and the guard's voice came through the speaker, telling them that he could see no one in the area. This was despite the fact that the original guard and the supervisor were looking right at the person on the security monitor.

The guard later recalled that the figure she had seen was wearing a white shirt with dark pants, a description that matched Frank Nash's clothing on the day of the massacre. The figure's missing head might be explained by the fact that, during the battle, Nash's head was nearly blown completely off, either by the hail of machine-gun fire or by the misfired shotgun from the backseat of the car. Other staff members and visitors have reportedly seen Nash's ghost, both with his head and without it, at several different locations in Union Station, both in the daytime and at night.

Does Frank Nash still lurk in the darkest corners of Kansas City's Union Station? And if he does, how long will he linger here? It seems very possible that his confused and tortured spirit has remained behind at the place where he met his tragic end, but how long he may stay here is a question that no one can answer.

Bibliography

Bearss, Edwin C. *The Battle of Wilson's Creek.* Springfield, MO: Wilson's Creek National Battlefield Foundation, 1985.

Burrough, Bryan. *Public Enemies.* New York: Penguin, 2004.

Cottrell, Steve. *Haunted Ozark Battlefields* (unpublished manuscript).

Courteway, Robbi. *Spirits of St. Louis.* St. Louis: Virginia Publishing, 1999.

Goodwin, David. *Ghosts of Jefferson Barracks.* Alton, IL: Whitechapel Press, 2001.

Kirschten, Ernest. *Catfish and Crystal.* New York: Doubleday, 1960.

Marley, Brant. *Jesse James.* New York: Berkley, 1998.

Medlin, Jarrett. "Haunted Hannibal." *Rural Missouri Magazine,* October 2006.

Nash, Jay Robert. *Bloodletters and Badmen.* New York: M. Evans and Company, 1995.

Offutt, Jason. *Haunted Missouri.* Kirksville, MO: Truman State University Press, 2007.

Piston, William Garrett, and Richard W. Hatcher III. *Wilson's Creek: The Second Battle of the Civil War and the Men Who Fought It.* Chapel Hill: The University of North Carolina Press, 2000.

Scott, Beth, and Michael Norman. *Haunted Heartland.* New York: Dorset Press, 1985.

Strait, James. *Weird Missouri.* New York: Sterling, 2008.

Taylor, Troy. *Beyond the Grave.* Alton, IL: Whitechapel Press, 2001.

———. *Dead Men Do Tell Tales.* Alton, IL: Whitechapel Press, 2008.

———. *Haunted St. Louis.* Alton, IL: Whitechapel Press, 2002.

———. *Haunting of America.* Chicago: Whitechapel Press, 2009.

———. *Suicide and Spirits.* Chicago: Whitechapel Press, 2011.

Tremear, Janice. *Missouri's Haunted Route 66.* Charleston, SC: History Press, 2010.

Wallace, Stone. *Dustbowl Desperadoes.* Edmonton, AB: Folklore Publishing, 2004.

Weaver, H. Dwight. *Missouri Caves in History and Legend.* Columbia: University of Missouri Press, 2008.

Winter, William C. *The Civil War in St. Louis.* St. Louis: Missouri Historical Society Press, 1994.

About the Author

TROY TAYLOR IS THE AUTHOR OF NEARLY SIXTY BOOKS ABOUT HISTORY, hauntings, crime, and the supernatural in America. He is the founder and president of the American Ghost Society and the owner of the Illinois and American Hauntings tour companies. Along with writing about the unusual and hosting tours, Taylor is also a public speaker on the subject of ghosts and hauntings and has appeared in newspaper and magazine articles about ghosts. He has been interviewed hundreds of times for radio and television broadcasts about the supernatural. He has also appeared in a number of documentary films, several television series, and in one feature film about the paranormal. He currently resides in central Illinois.

Other Titles by Troy Taylor

The Big Book of Illinois Ghost Stories
978-0-8117-0504-2

Monsters of Illinois
978-0-8117-3640-4

Haunted Illinois
978-0-8117-3499-8

WWW.STACKPOLEBOOKS.COM
1-800-732-3669

Other Titles in the
Haunted Series

Haunted Arizona
by Charles A. Stansfield Jr. • 978-0-8117-3620-6

Haunted Colorado
by Charles A. Stansfield Jr. • 978-0-8117-0855-5

Haunted Connecticut
by Cheri Revai • 978-0-8117-3296-3

Haunted Delaware
by Patricia A. Martinelli • 978-0-8117-3297-0

Haunted Florida
by Cynthia Thuma & Catherine Lower
978-0-8117-3498-1

Haunted Georgia
by Alan Brown • 978-0-8117-3443-1

Haunted Hudson Valley
by Cheri Farnsworth • 978-0-8117-3621-3

Haunted Indiana
by James A. Willis • 978-0-8117-0779-4

Haunted Jersey Shore
by Charles A. Stansfield Jr. • 978-0-8117-3267-3

Haunted Kentucky
by Alan Brown • 978-0-8117-3584-1

Haunted Maine
by Charles A. Stansfield Jr. • 978-0-8117-3373-1

Haunted Maryland
by Ed Okonowicz • 978-0-8117-3409-7

Haunted Massachusetts
by Cheri Revai • 978-0-8117-3221-5

Haunted New Jersey
by Patricia A. Martinelli &
Charles A. Stansfield Jr.
978-0-8117-3156-0

WWW.STACKPOLEBOOKS.COM • 1-800-732-3669

Other Titles in the
Haunted Series

Haunted New York
by Cheri Revai • 978-0-8117-3249-9

Haunted New York City
by Cheri Revai • 978-0-8117-3471-4

Haunted North Carolina
by Patty A. Wilson • 978-0-8117-3585-8

Haunted Northern California
by Charles A. Stansfield Jr. • 978-0-8117-3586-5

Haunted Ohio
by Charles A. Stansfield Jr. • 978-0-8117-3472-1

Haunted Pennsylvania
by Mark Nesbitt & Patty A. Wilson • 978-0-8117-3298-7

Haunted South Carolina
by Alan Brown • 978-0-8117-3635-0

Haunted Southern California
by Charles A. Stansfield Jr. • 978-0-8117-3539-1

Haunted Tennessee
by Alan Brown • 978-0-8117-3540-7

Haunted Texas
by Alan Brown • 978-0-8117-3500-1

Haunted Vermont
by Charles A. Stansfield Jr. • 978-0-8117-3399-1

Haunted Virginia
by L. B. Taylor Jr. • 978-0-8117-3541-4

Haunted Washington
by Charles A. Stansfield Jr. • 978-0-8117-0683-4

Haunted West Virginia
by Patty A. Wilson • 978-0-8117-3400-4

Haunted Wisconsin
by Linda S. Godfrey • 978-0-8117-3636-7

WWW.STACKPOLEBOOKS.COM • 1-800-732-3669